ADULT ALL-IN-ONE COURSE
LESSON · THEORY · SOLO

T0044706

FOREWORD

With the goal of teaching the adult beginner to play the piano in an enjoyable, quick and easy way, Alfred's Basic Adult All-in-One Course, Level 2, continues to progress smoothly and easily, without gaps, toward the development of technique and knowledge required to play in all the most frequently used keys. This book begins with a review of the chords and keys previously studied, using fresh and interesting material that will provide enjoyment as well as reinforcement. Particularly significant and noteworthy is the easy presentation of chords in all positions in both hands.

The pieces used in this book consist of familiar favorites borrowed from folk-song material, themes from operas and the classics, as well as original keyboard compositions.

At the completion of this book, the student will be ready to begin Alfred's Adult All-in-One Course, Level 3 (14540). Upon completion of the entire course, the student will have learned to play some of the most popular music ever written and will have gained a thorough understanding of the basic concepts of music.

Willard A. Palmer
Morton Manus
Amanda Vick Lethco

A General MIDI disk (14428) and CD (14532)
are available, both of which offer a full piano
recording and background accompaniment.

Copyright © MCMXCV by Alfred Publishing Co., Inc.
All rights reserved. Printed in USA.
ISBN 0-88284-995-6

Cover photo: Jeff Oshiro

CONTENTS

Review—The Key of C Major

Primary Chords in C Major:

Block chords

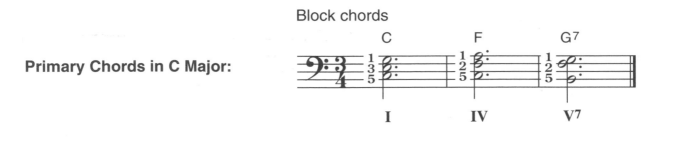

Broken chords

DOWN IN THE VALLEY 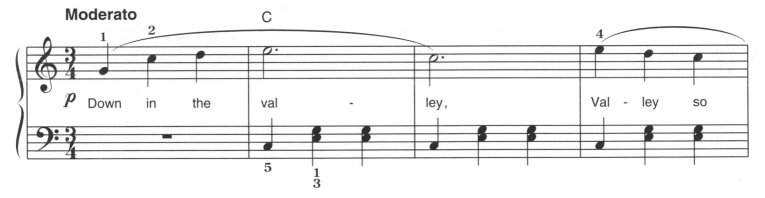 *

American Folk Song

Moderato

p Down in the val - ley, Val - ley so

low, Late in the eve -

┌EXTENDED POSITION┐

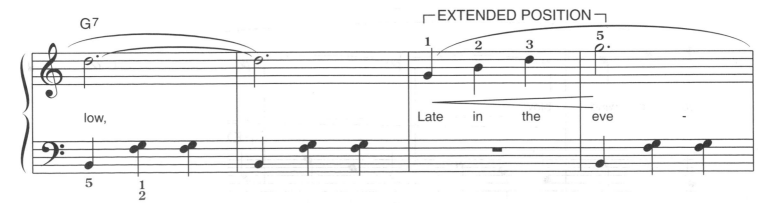

* This symbol indicates the track number of the selection on the CD. See the General MIDI (GM) disk sleeve for the GM track numbers.

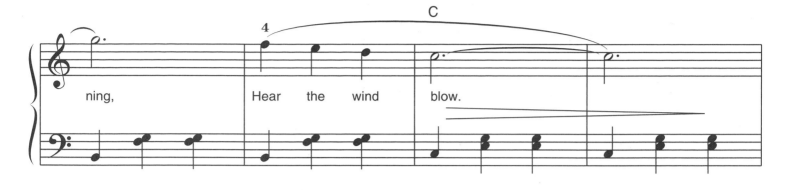

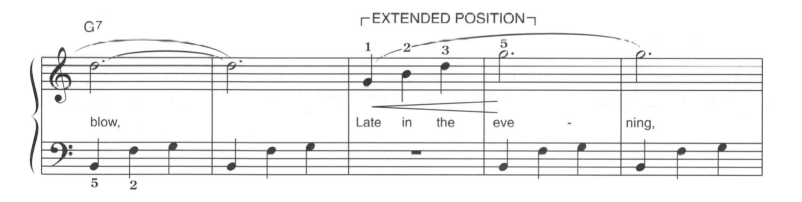

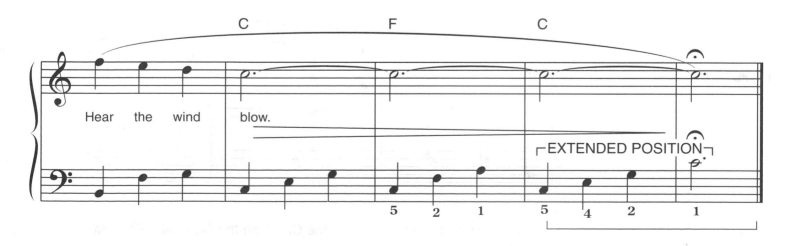

Review—Chords in the Key of C Major

KEY SIGNATURE: NO SHARPS, NO FLATS

REMEMBER: When moving from one chord to another it usually sounds best to keep a COMMON TONE between neighboring chords, to make a smooth progression.

In LEVEL ONE, you learned that you can move from the root position of the **I** CHORD of any MAJOR KEY by keeping the lowest note as a COMMON TONE between **I** & **IV**, and the highest note as a COMMON TONE between **I** & **V**^{7}.

In the KEY OF C MAJOR, this works as follows:

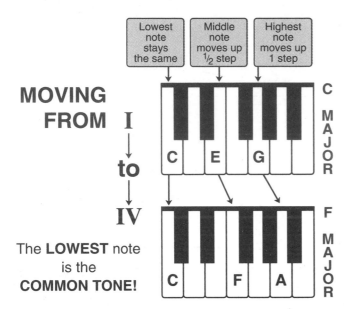

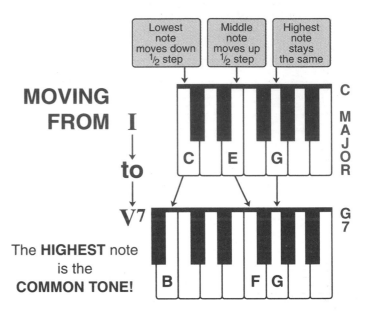

C is the COMMON TONE between **I** & **IV**.   **G** is the COMMON TONE between **I** & **V**^{7}.

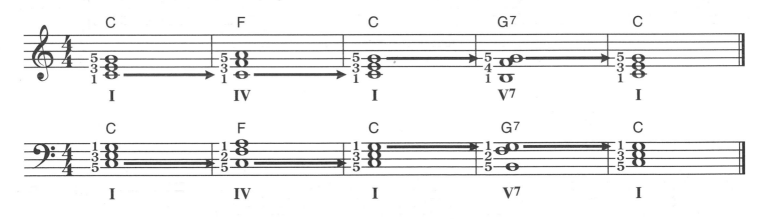

1. Rewrite the above progressions on the following staffs.
2. Add fingering.   3. Add arrows to show the common tones.   4. Play with hands separate.

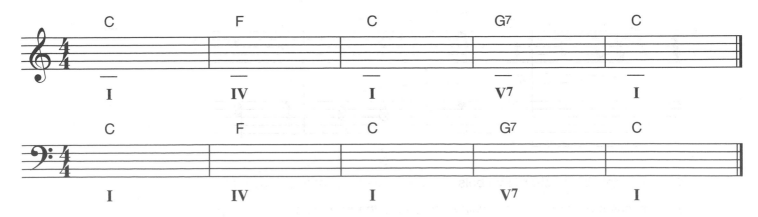

BRIDAL CHORUS from "Lohengrin"

Richard Wagner

*IMPORTANT! In this book, chord symbols are used only to identify chords that have been previously introduced.

**D. C. al Fine means *repeat from the beginning, and play to the Fine (end).*

LH Extended Positions (Note Reading Review)

Each of the following lines is played with a LH EXTENDED POSITION beginning on a different note.

1. Write the names of the notes in the boxes.
2. Play. Use the damper pedal as indicated.

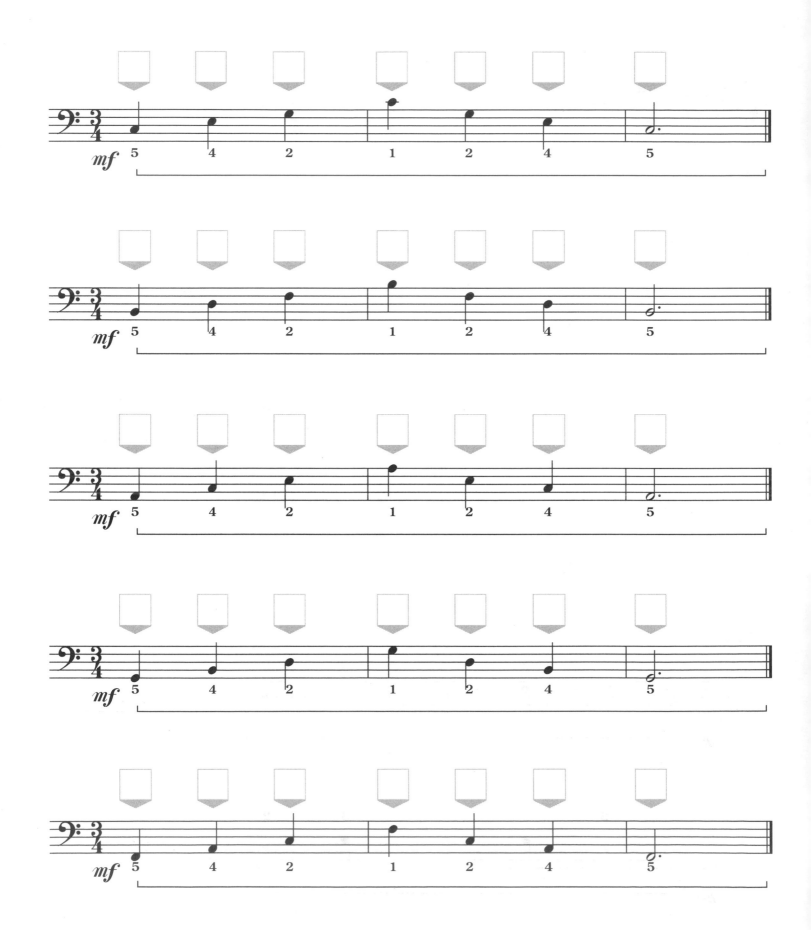

RH Extended Positions (Note Reading Review)

Each of the following lines is played with a RH EXTENDED POSITION beginning on a different note.

1. Write the names of the notes in the boxes.
2. Play. Use the damper pedal as indicated.

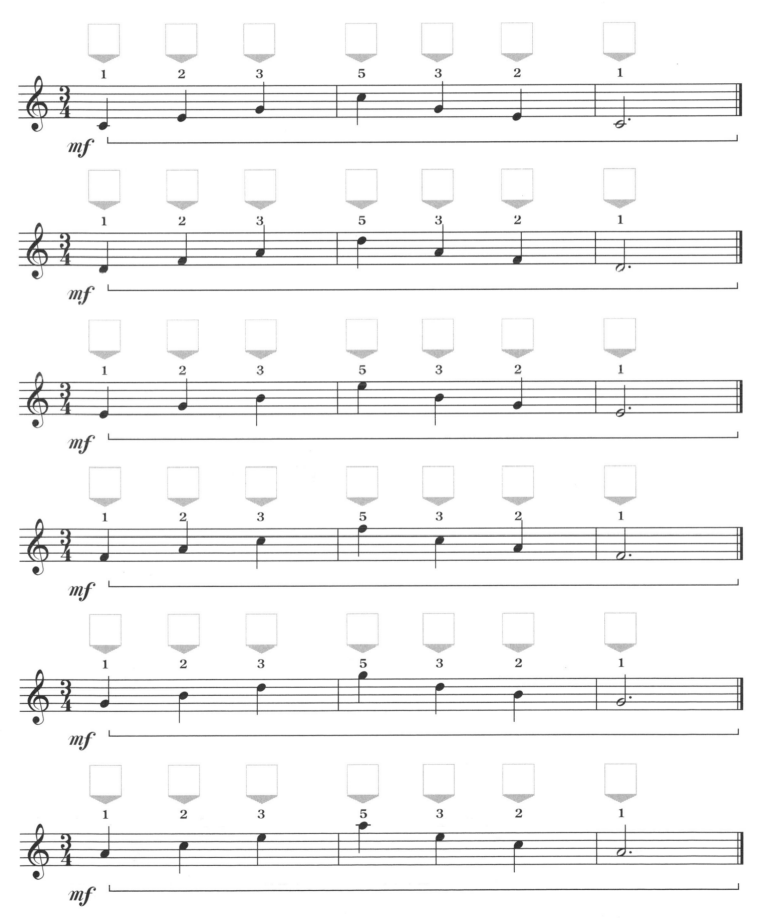

GUANTANAMERA

Traditional

Moderately slow

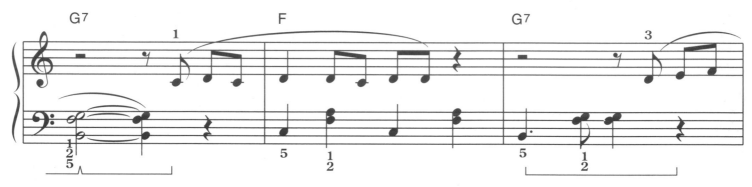

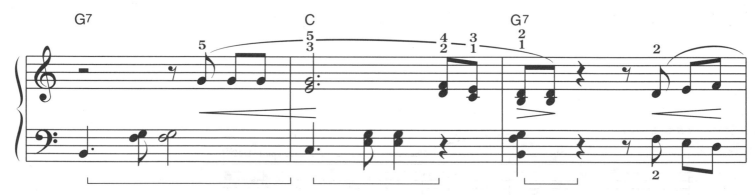

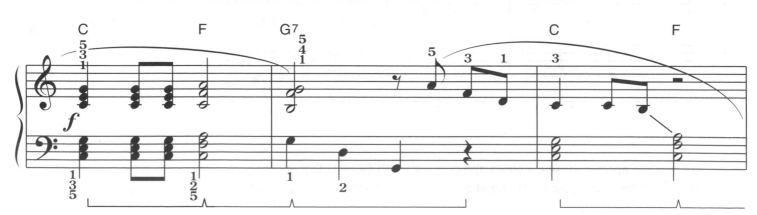

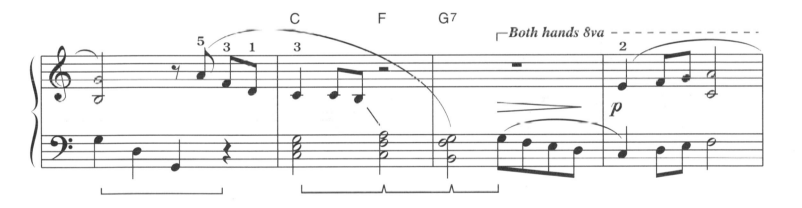

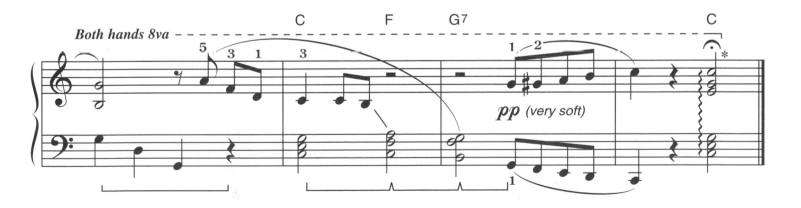

* When a wavy line appears beside a chord, the chord is ARPEGGIATED (broken or rolled). Play the lowest note first, and quickly add the next higher notes one at a time until the chord is complete. The first note is played on the beat.

Review—Chords in the Key of A Minor

KEY SIGNATURE: NO SHARPS, NO FLATS (relative of C MAJOR).

When you move from the root position of the i chord in any MINOR KEY, you also keep the lowest note as a COMMON TONE between i & iv, and the highest note as a COMMON TONE between i and V⁷. You should carefully note how the other tones move.

In the KEY OF A MINOR this works as follows:

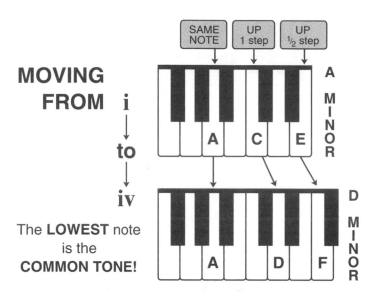

A is the COMMON TONE between i & iv.

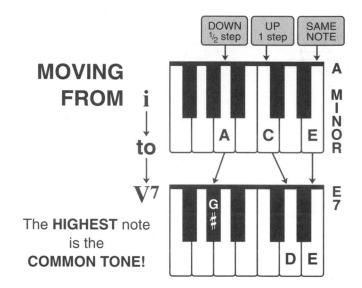

E is the COMMON TONE between i & V⁷.

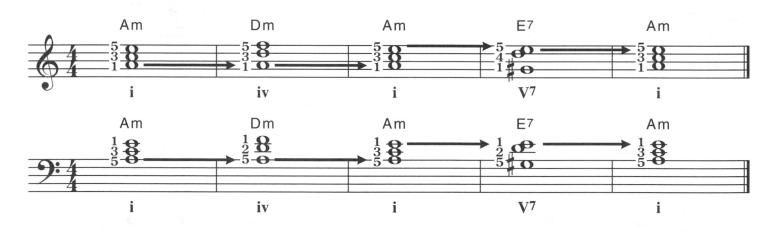

1. Rewrite the above progressions on the following staffs.
2. Add fingering. 3. Add arrows to show the common tones. 4. Play with hands separate.

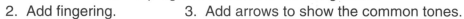

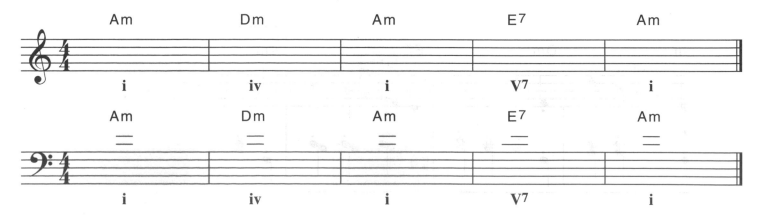

Theme from the OVERTURE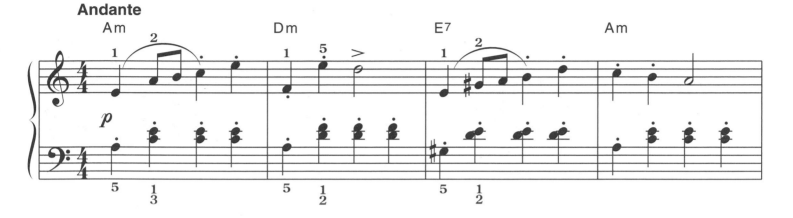

(from the opera "Raymond")

> **KEY OF A MINOR**
> Key Signature: No ♯'s, no ♭'s

Ambroise Thomas

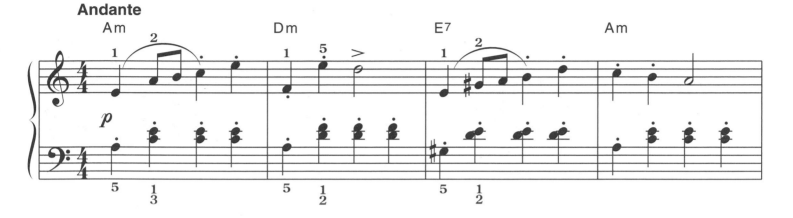

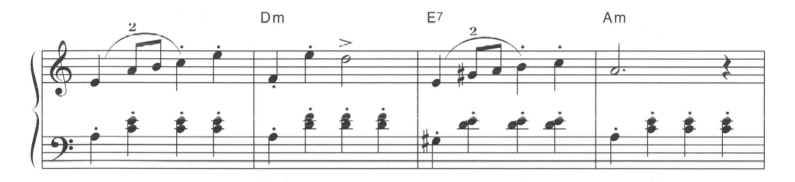

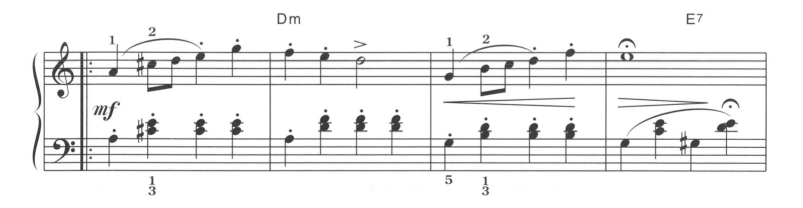

Technic Builder: Passing 1 Under 2

It is important to develop the ability to pass 1 under 2 and 1 under 3 with a relaxed wrist, and with no "twisting" motion of the hand. The next six pages of this book will help you improve this technic. Play the exercises slowly at first, then faster.

1. Write the finger numbers OVER each of the following notes, passing 1 under 2, as shown in the first example.
2. Write the names of the notes in the boxes, then play with the RH.

3. Write the finger numbers UNDER each of the following notes, passing 1 under 2, as shown in the first example.
4. Write the names of the notes in the boxes, then play with the LH.

Technic Builder: Passing 1 Under 3

1. Write the finger numbers OVER each of the following notes, passing 1 under 3, as shown in the first example.
2. Write the names of the notes in the boxes. If a note is sharp, include the sharp in the box.
3. Play with RH.

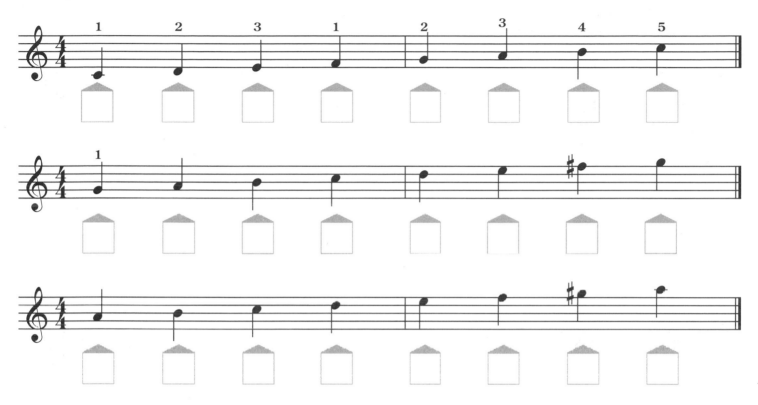

4. Write the finger numbers UNDER each of the following notes, passing 1 under 3, as shown in the first example.
5. Write the names of the notes in the boxes. Include any sharps that are needed.
6. Play with LH.

LIGHT AND BLUE

Willard A. Palmer

Moderate blues tempo

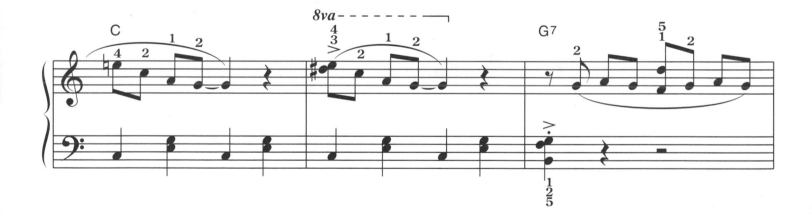

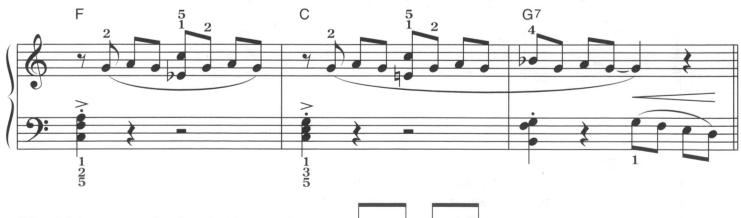

*The eighth notes may be played a bit unevenly:

long   short long   short, *etc.*

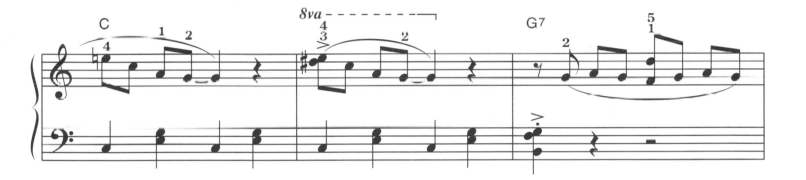

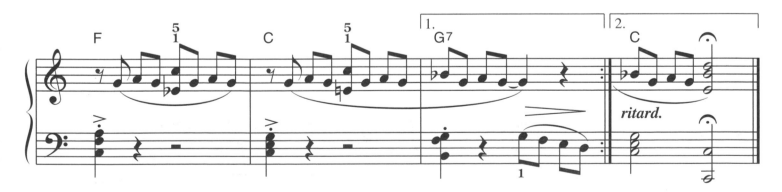

TEACHER'S NOTE:
1. The LH may be played *staccato*, except where slurred.
2. The repeat may be played *8va*, with notes marked *8va* played as written.
3. The final chord may be played with *tremolo:*

Hungarian Rhapsody No. 2
(Theme)

Not too fast, with rhythmic emphasis

Franz Liszt

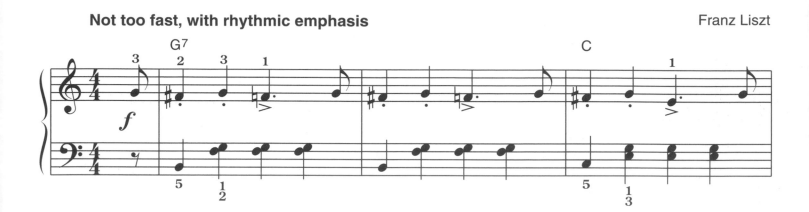

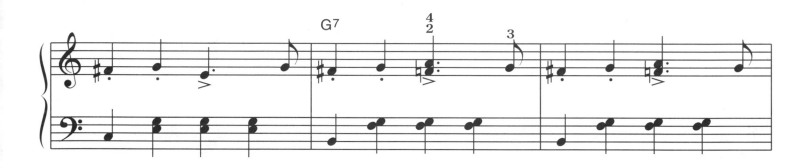

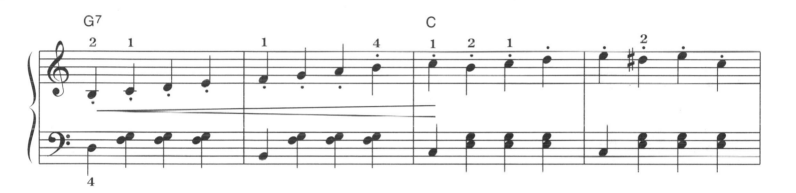

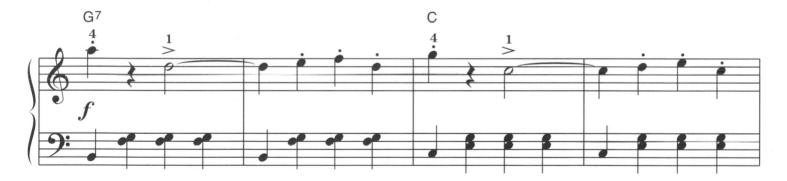

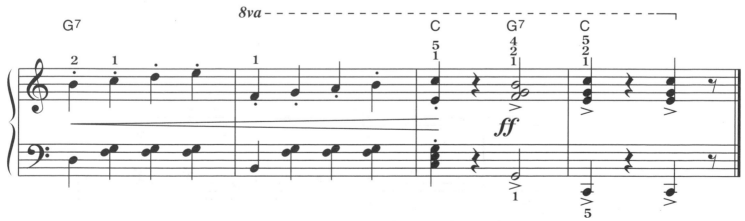

You are now ready to begin GREATEST HITS, Level 2.

Review—The Key of F Major

KEY SIGNATURE: 1 FLAT (B♭)

Primary Chords in F Major:

Block chords

Broken chords

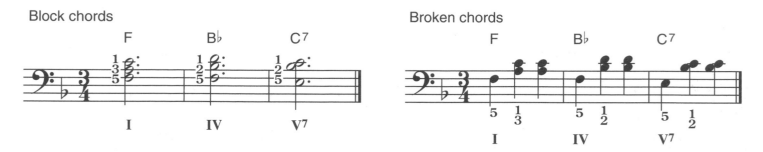

F is the COMMON TONE BETWEEN **I** & **IV**.   C is the COMMON TONE BETWEEN **I** & **V**⁷.

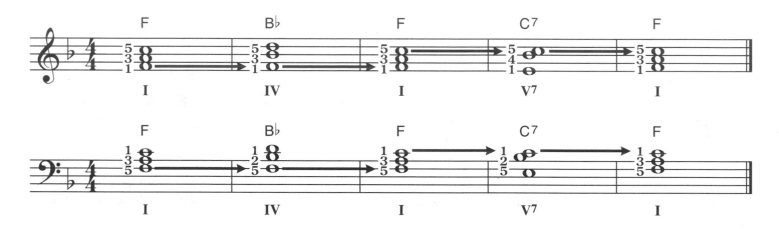

MORNING HAS BROKEN

KEY OF F MAJOR
Key Signature: 1 flat (B♭)

Gaelic Folk Song

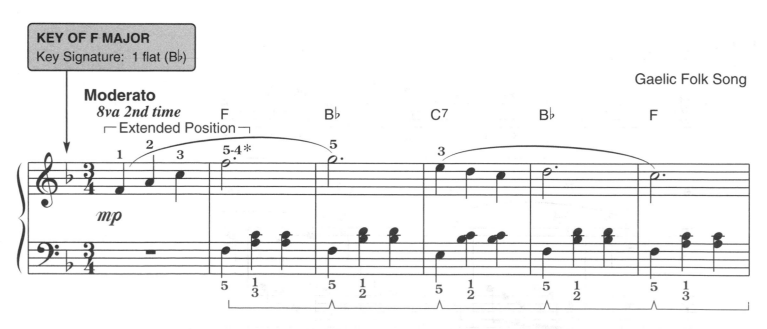

*Play with 5, then change to 4 while holding the key down. This is called "finger substitution."

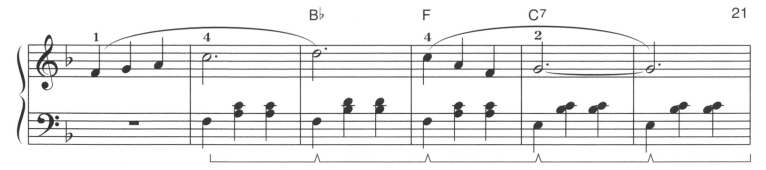

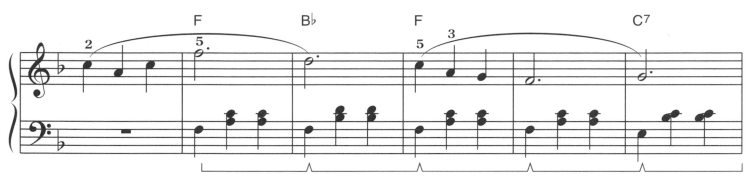

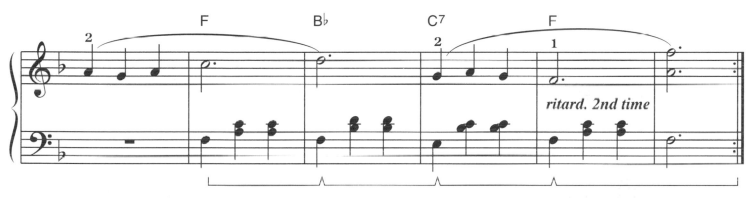

Most popular sheet music has chord symbols above the treble notes just as you can see in *MORNING HAS BROKEN*. You may supply your own LH chords to such music, using BLOCK CHORDS or BROKEN CHORDS in various styles.

OPTIONAL: Play *MORNING HAS BROKEN* again, using broken chords as shown in the following examples. The chords you use should be the same as those indicated by the chord symbols above the treble notes in the music above.

Example 1:

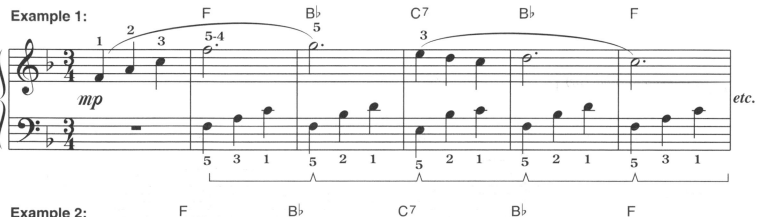

Example 2:

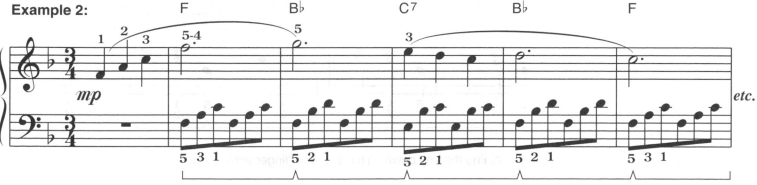

ALEXANDER'S RAGTIME BAND

Irving Berlin

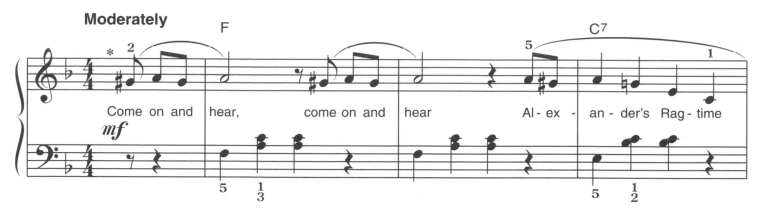

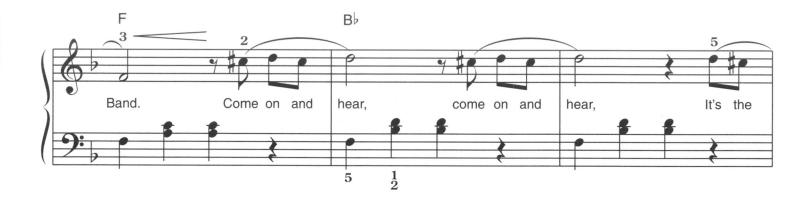

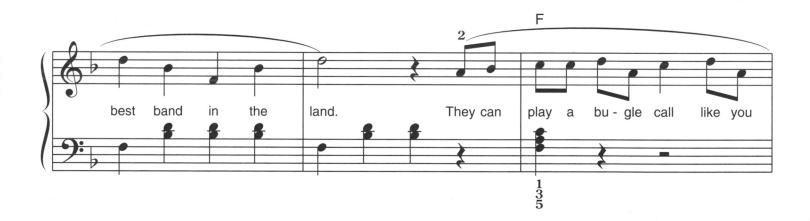

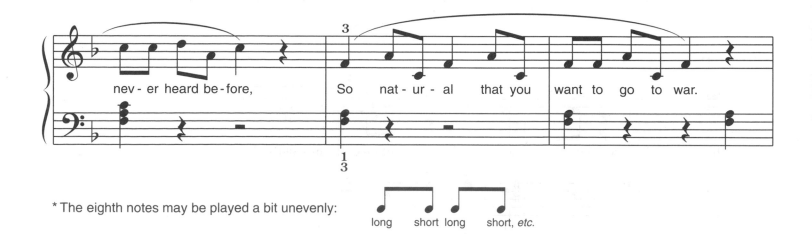

* The eighth notes may be played a bit unevenly:

long   short long   short, *etc.*

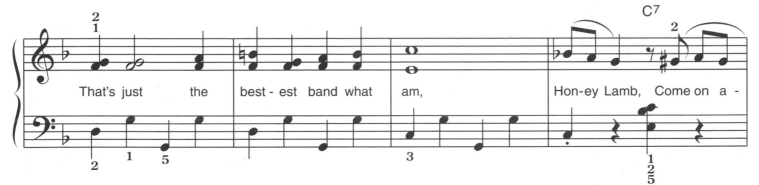

That's just the best-est band what am, Hon-ey Lamb, Come on a-

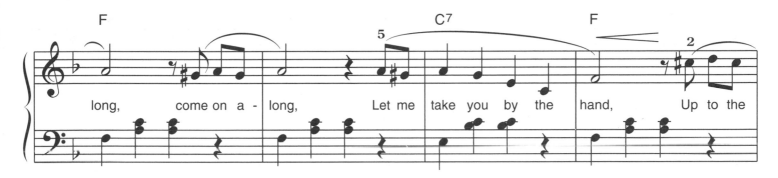

long, come on a-long, Let me take you by the hand, Up to the

man, up to the man who's the lead-er of the band, And if you

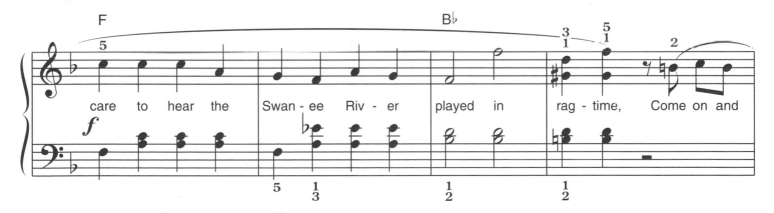

care to hear the Swan-ee Riv-er played in rag-time, Come on and

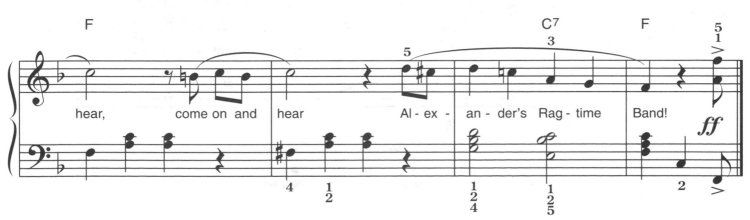

hear, come on and hear Al-ex-an-der's Rag-time Band!

Theme from SOLACE
(A Mexican Serenade)

Very slow march time

Scott Joplin

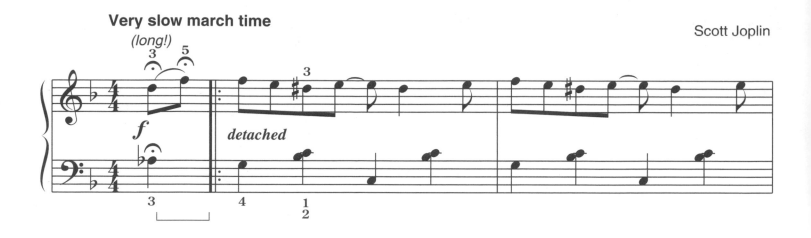

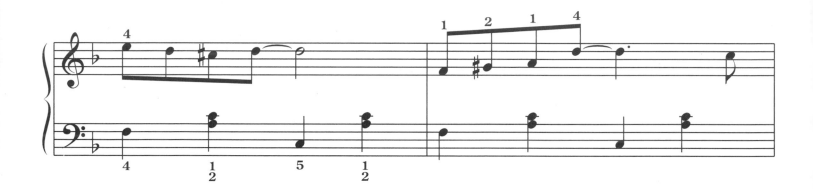

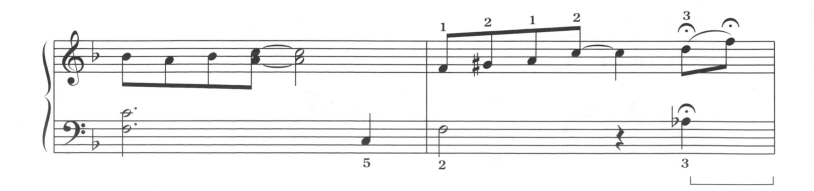

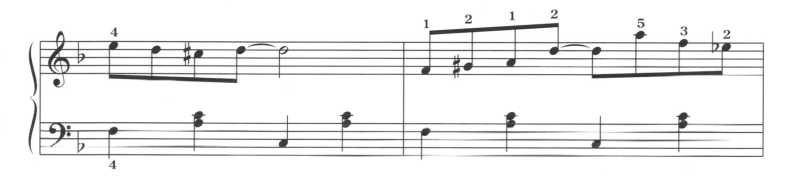

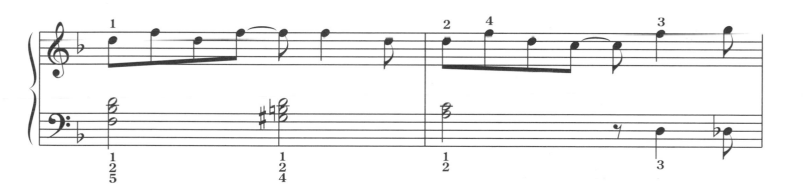

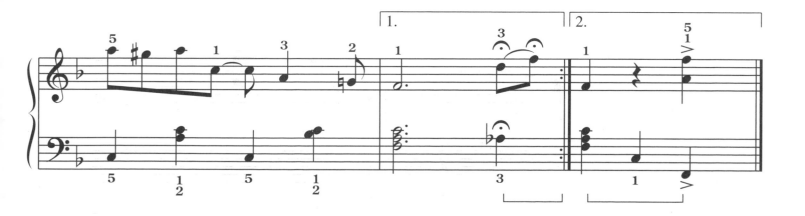

La Bamba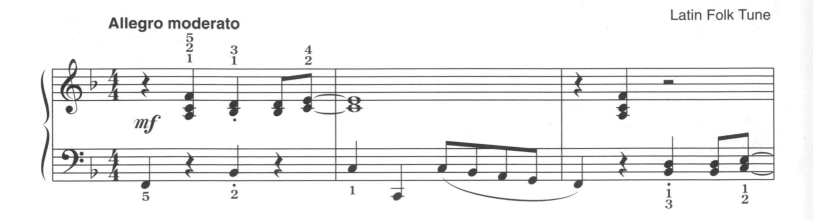

Latin Folk Tune

Allegro moderato

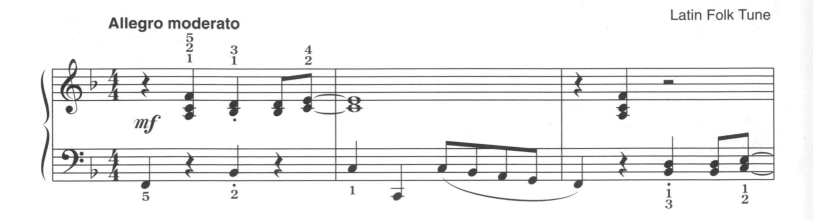

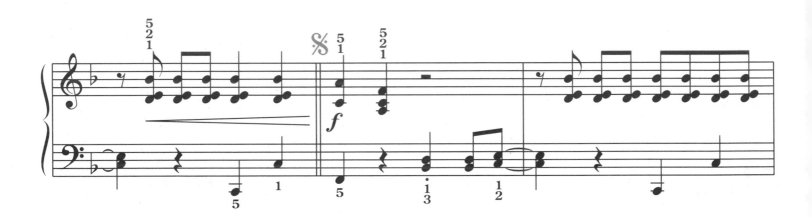

D. S. 𝄋 *al* ⊕*, then CODA**

⊕ **CODA**

Repeat and fade

*D. S. (dal segno) means *repeat from the sign.*

D. S. 𝄋 *al* ⊕*, then CODA* means *repeat from the sign* 𝄋*, play to the Coda sign* ⊕*, then play the CODA.*

A New Time Signature

6/8

means **6** beats to each measure.

means an **eighth note** gets 1 beat.

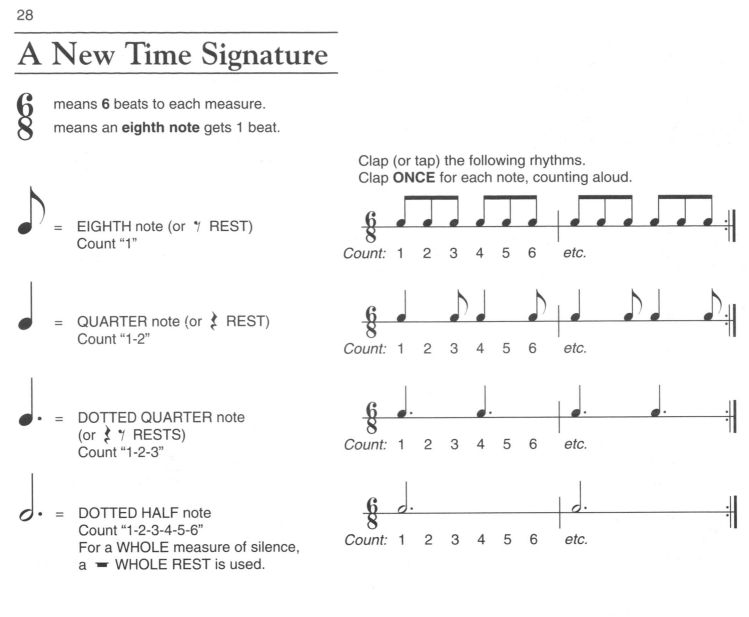

♪ = EIGHTH note (or ♪ REST)
Count "1"

♩ = QUARTER note (or ⸶ REST)
Count "1-2"

♩. = DOTTED QUARTER note
(or ⸶ ♪ RESTS)
Count "1-2-3"

♩. = DOTTED HALF note
Count "1-2-3-4-5-6"
For a WHOLE measure of silence,
a ▬ WHOLE REST is used.

Clap (or tap) the following rhythms.
Clap **ONCE** for each note, counting aloud.

Count: 1 2 3 4 5 6   etc.

Count: 1 2 3 4 5 6   etc.

Count: 1 2 3 4 5 6   etc.

Count: 1 2 3 4 5 6   etc.

LA RASPA

A Mexican Stamping Dance

KEY OF F MAJOR
Key Signature: 1 flat (B♭)

Allegro
*2nd time accelerando poco a poco al fine**

Latin Folk Tune

* *Accelerando* means *gradually faster.*   *Poco a poco* means *little by little.*

    Accelerando poco a poco al fine means *gradually faster little by little to the end.*

D. C. al Fine

* *sf* = *sforzando*, Italian for "forcing." It means *to play louder on one note or chord;* in this case
it applies to the note above *sf* and the chord below it.

6/8 Time Signature

In 6/8 time:

1. How many counts does an eighth note get? Answer: _____

2. How many counts does a QUARTER note get? _____

3. How many counts does a DOTTED QUARTER note get? _____

4. How many counts does a DOTTED HALF note get? _____

5. How many counts does this rest (♪) get? _____

6. How many counts does this rest (𝄽) get? _____

7. How many total counts do these rests (𝄽 ♪) get? _____

8. What kind of rest means REST FOR A WHOLE MEASURE? _____

FOR HE'S A JOLLY GOOD FELLOW

9. Add bar lines. The incomplete measures are completed at the end of each section.

10. Play.

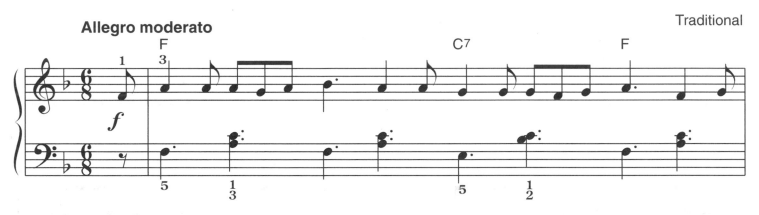

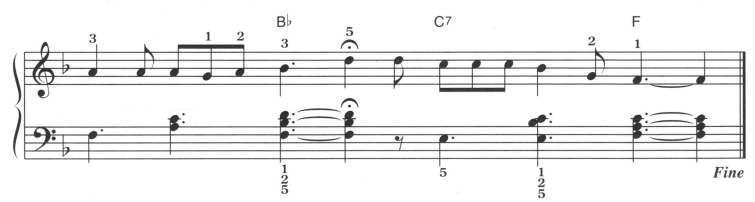

D. C. al Fine

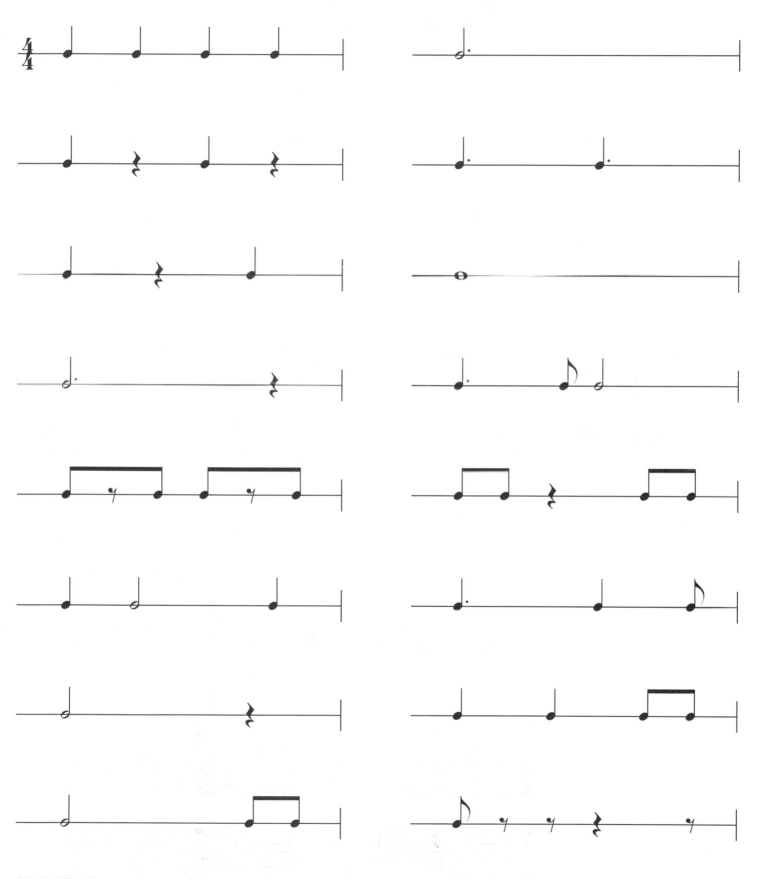 31

Review—Time Signatures

Each of the following examples represents just ONE MEASURE of music.

1. Write the TIME SIGNATURE at the beginning of each line, as shown in the first example.
2. COUNT ALOUD and TAP (or CLAP) once for each note.

SCORE 10 for each correct time signature.   Perfect score = 150   **YOUR SCORE:** _____

MEXICAN HAT DANCE

Traditional

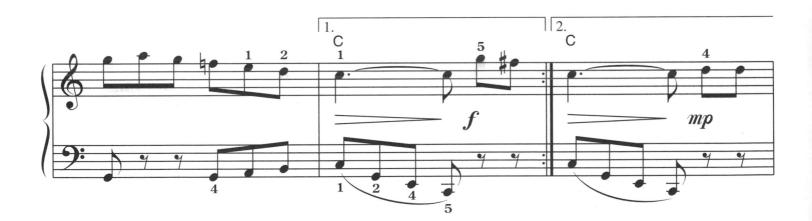

*Play the F and G together with the side of the thumb.

Review—The Key of D Minor

KEY SIGNATURE: 1 FLAT (B♭) (relative of F MAJOR).

D is the COMMON TONE between **i** & **iv**. **A** is the COMMON TONE between **i** & **V⁷**.

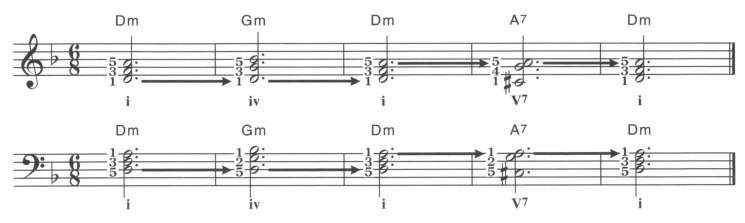

1. Rewrite the above progressions on the following staffs.
2. Add fingering.   3. Add arrows to show the common tones.   4. Play with hands separate.

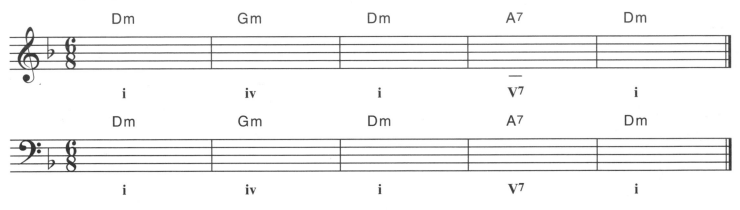

TARANTELLA

5. Add bar lines. The incomplete measure is completed at the end.
6. Play.

FESTIVE DANCE

KEY OF D MINOR
Key Signature: 1 flat (B♭)

Allegro*
2nd time 8va, last time loco (as written, not 8va)

mf

LH staccato

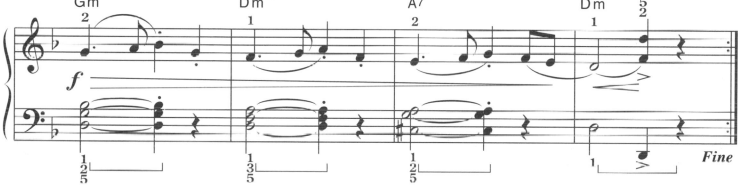

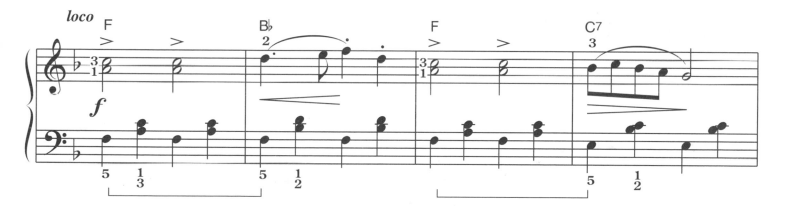

D. C. al Fine

*It is also very effective to begin this piece very slowly and play gradually faster and faster to the end.

SCHERZO*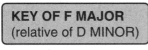

Respectfully dedicated to the memory of world-renowned concert pianist, Vladimir Horowitz.

KEY OF D MINOR
Key Signature: 1 flat (B♭)

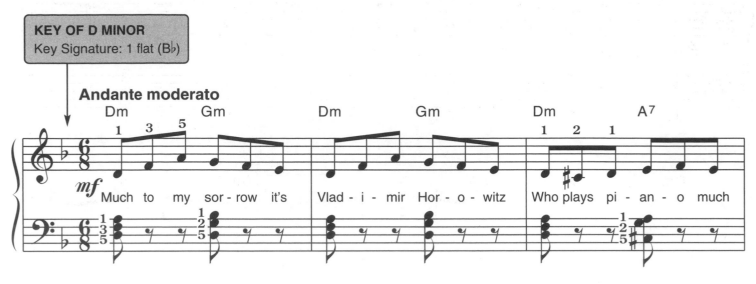

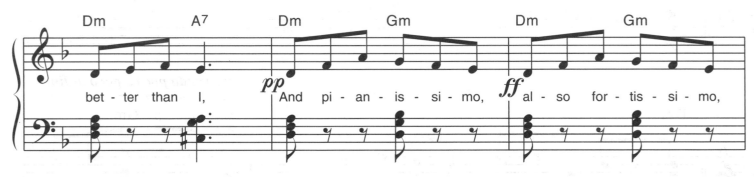

KEY OF F MAJOR
(relative of D MINOR)

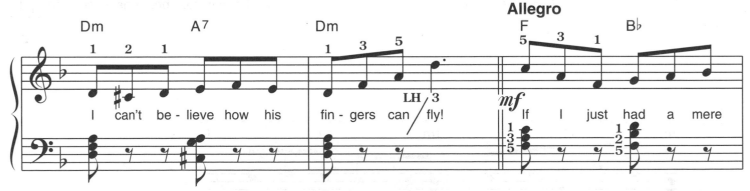

---

*__Scherzo.__ This word means *a musical jest or joke.* It is applied to light and playful pieces.

KEY OF D MINOR

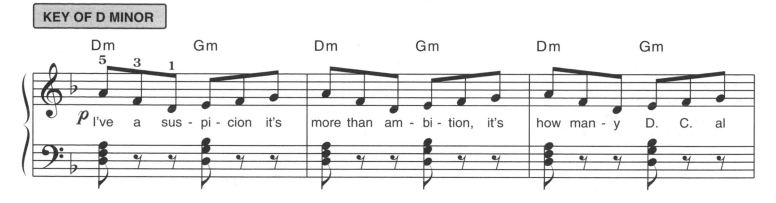

I've a sus-pi-cion it's more than am-bi-tion, it's how man-y D. C. al

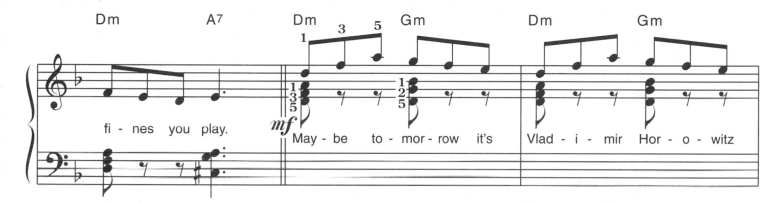

fi-nes you play.   May-be to-mor-row it's Vlad-i-mir Hor-o-witz

accelerando poco a poco al fine
Both hands 8va - - - - - - - - - -

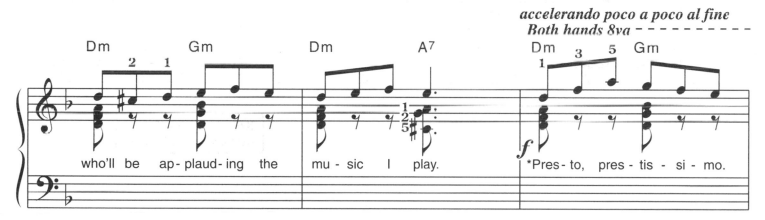

who'll be ap-plaud-ing the mu-sic I play.   *Pres-to, pres-tis-si-mo.

(Both hands 8va) - - - - - - - - - -

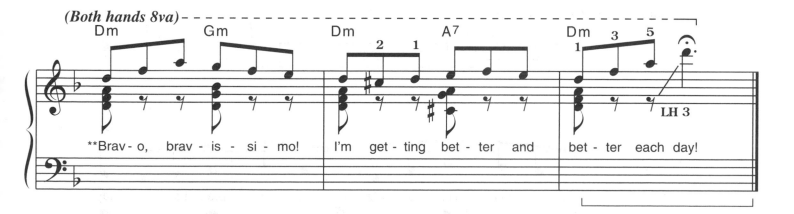

**Brav-o, brav-is-si-mo!   I'm get-ting bet-ter and bet-ter each day!

---

* ***Presto.*** Italian for "fast." This tempo mark means *faster than* **allegro.**
     The word **prestissimo** means *very fast.* It usually means *as fast as possible.*

** ***Bravo, bravissimo!***   These Italian words are often shouted by audiences of virtuoso performers. They can't
     be exactly translated, but they mean something like *Marvelous, VERY marvelous!*

INTRODUCTION AND DANCE

This very popular folk tune uses mostly the primary chords in D MINOR, but you will also find two D MAJOR TRIADS, plus the **V⁷** and **I** chords in A MINOR and F MAJOR.

The popular song *"Those Were the Days"* was based on this old folk melody.

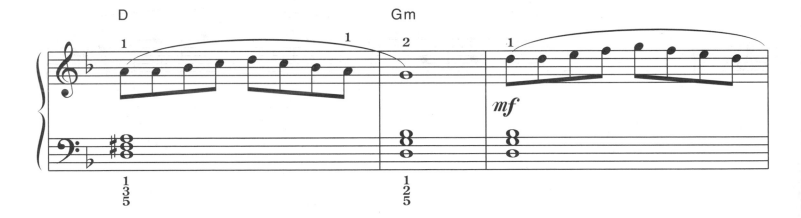

*The time signature **C** indicates COMMON TIME, which is the same as $\frac{4}{4}$ TIME.

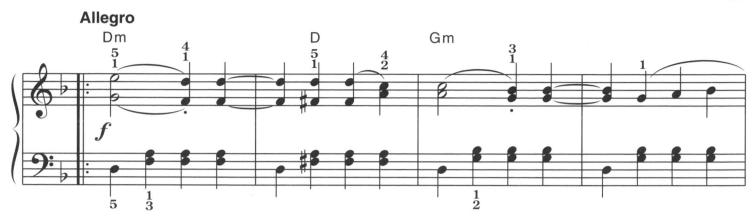

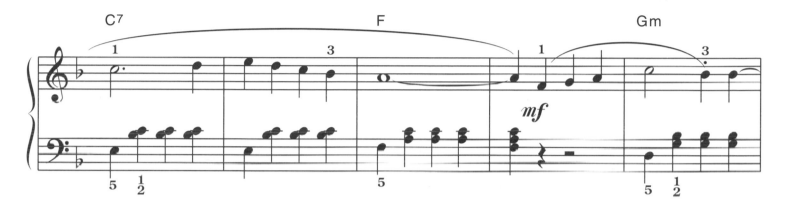

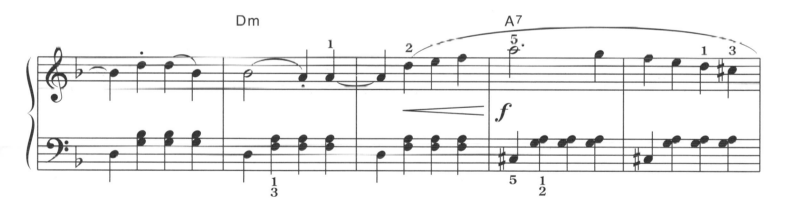

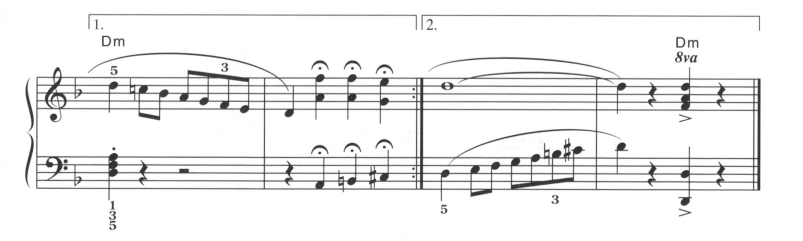

Review—The Key of G Major

KEY SIGNATURE: 1 SHARP (F♯)

G is the COMMON TONE between **I** & **IV**.   **D** is the COMMON TONE between **I** & **V⁷**.

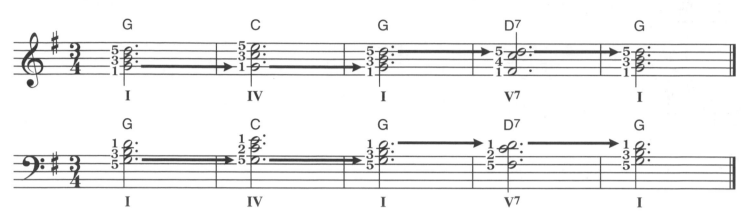

1. Rewrite the above progressions on the following staffs.
2. Add fingering.   3. Add arrows to show the common tones.   4. Play with hands separate.

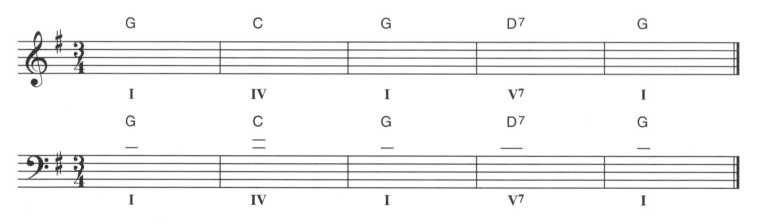

More About Extended Positions

EXTENDED POSITIONS often skip a 3rd between the first, second and third fingers, and a 4th between the third and fifth fingers. Sometimes they skip a 4th between the first and second fingers.

1. Write the names of the notes in the boxes.
2. Play, carefully observing the intervals between the notes.

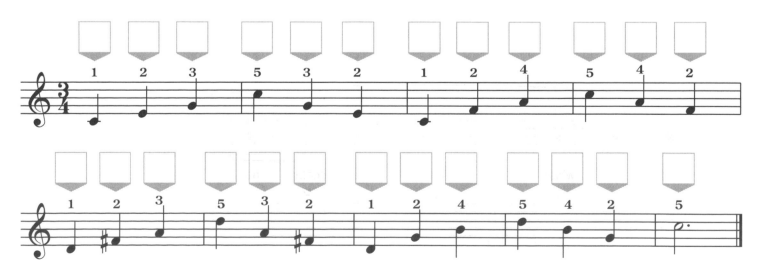

THE STREETS OF LAREDO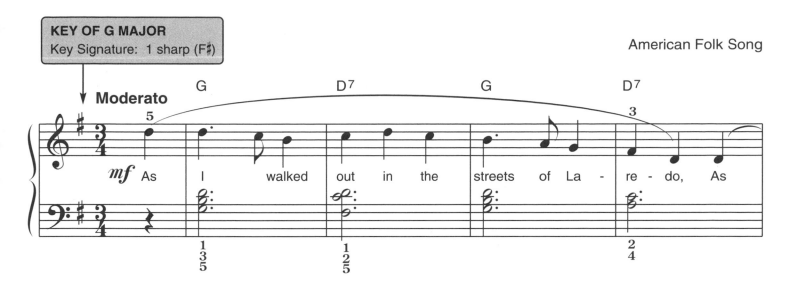

American Folk Song

KEY OF G MAJOR
Key Signature: 1 sharp (F♯)

Moderato

mf As I walked out in the streets of La - re - do, As

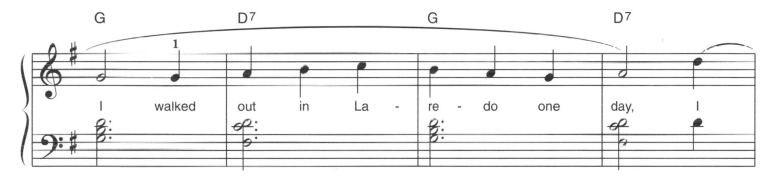

I walked out in La - re - do one day, I

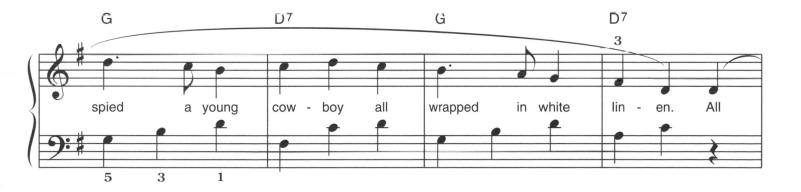

spied a young cow - boy all wrapped in white lin - en. All

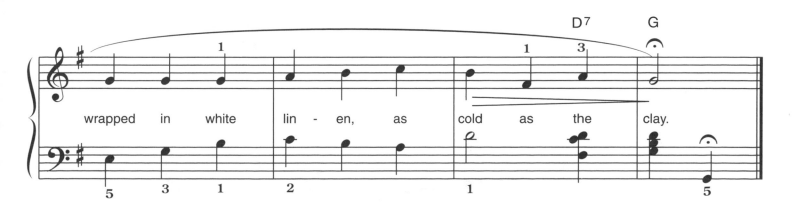

wrapped in white lin - en, as cold as the clay.

PLAISIR D'AMOUR

(The Joy of Love)

This piece was made into a popular song by Elvis Presley.

Giovanni Martini

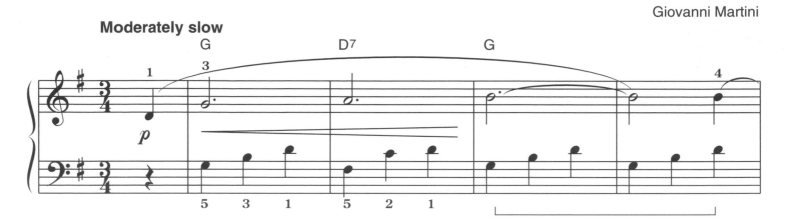

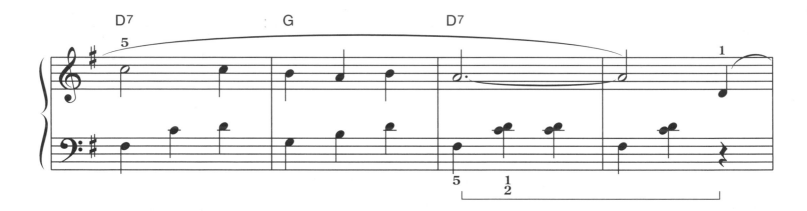

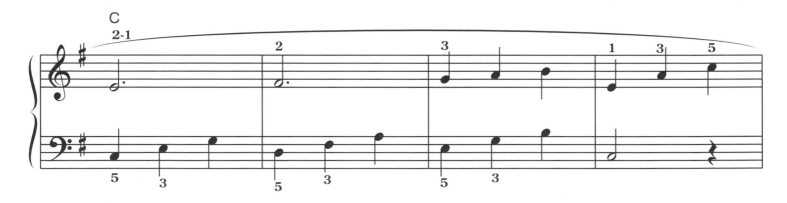

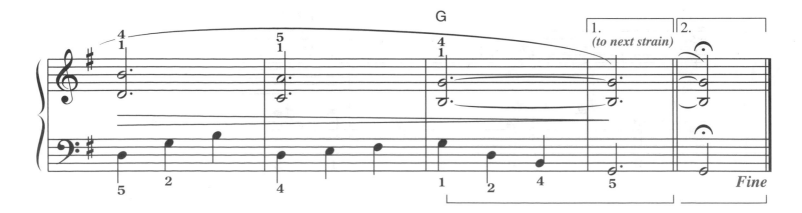

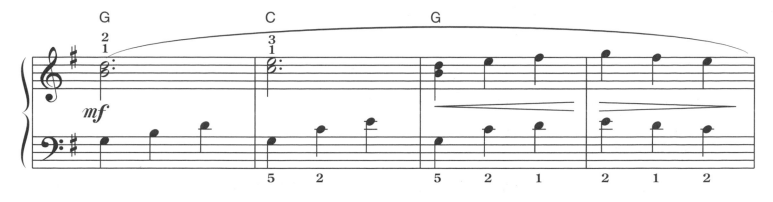

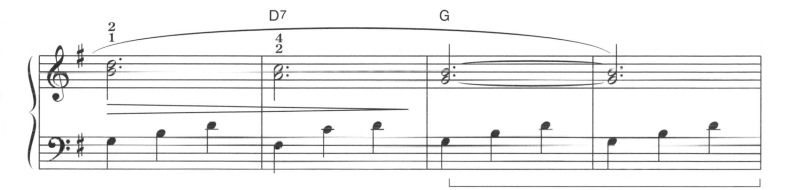

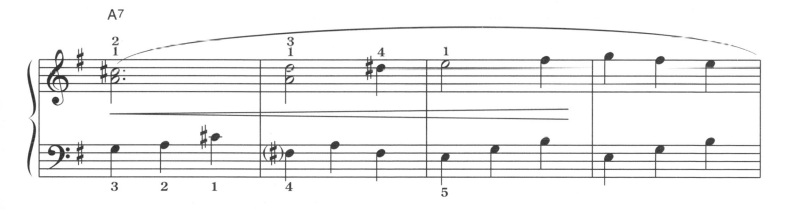

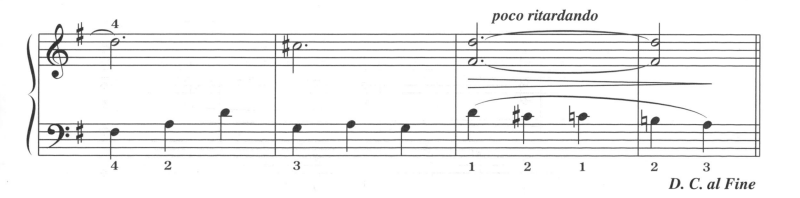

D. C. al Fine

44

The Key of E Minor (Relative of G Major)

E MINOR is the relative of **G MAJOR.**

Both keys have the same key signature (1 sharp, F♯).
REMEMBER: The RELATIVE MINOR begins on the 6th tone of the MAJOR SCALE.

G MAJOR SCALE

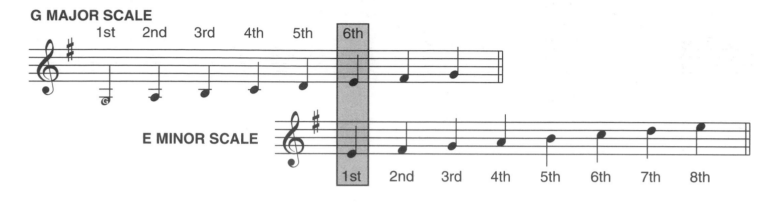

The minor scale shown above is the NATURAL MINOR SCALE.
The natural minor uses only notes that are found in the relative major scale.

The E Harmonic Minor Scale

In the HARMONIC MINOR SCALE, the 7th tone is raised ascending and descending.

The raised 7th in the key of E MINOR is D♯. It is not included in the key signature,
but is written as an "accidental" sharp each time it occurs.

Practice the E HARMONIC MINOR SCALE with hands separate. Begin slowly.

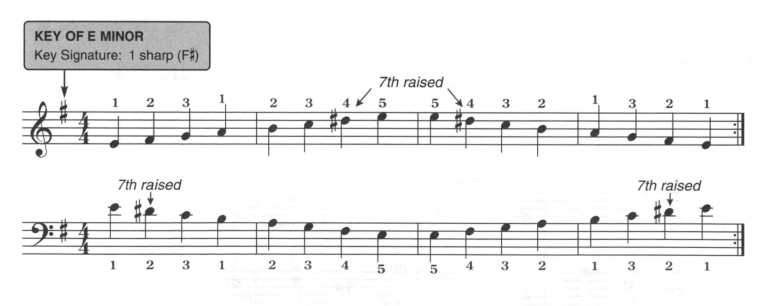

IMPORTANT! After you have learned the E HARMONIC MINOR SCALE with hands separate, you may
play the hands together in CONTRARY MOTION, by combining the two staffs above.
Notice that both hands play the same numbered fingers at the same time! Begin with
both thumbs on the same E.

THE HOUSE OF THE RISING SUN

Folk Song

KEY OF E MINOR
Key Signature: 1 sharp (F♯)

Andante moderato
2nd time both hands 8va

Ped. simile = Continue to pedal in the same manner.

The Primary Chords in E Minor

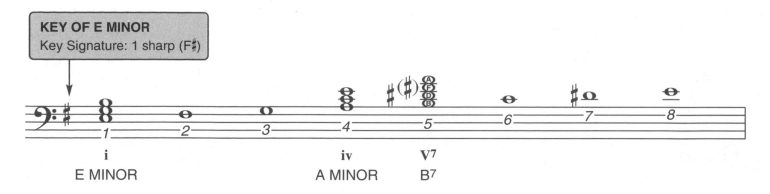

KEY OF E MINOR
Key Signature: 1 sharp (F♯)

i   iv   V⁷

E MINOR   A MINOR   B⁷

These positions are often used for smooth progressions:

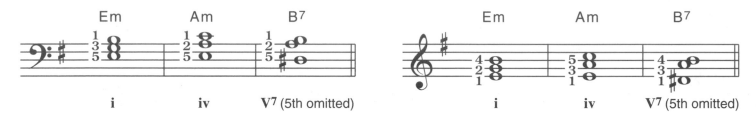

i   iv   V⁷ (5th omitted)   i   iv   V⁷ (5th omitted)

E is the COMMON TONE between **i** & **iv**. **B** is the COMMON TONE between **i** & **V⁷**.

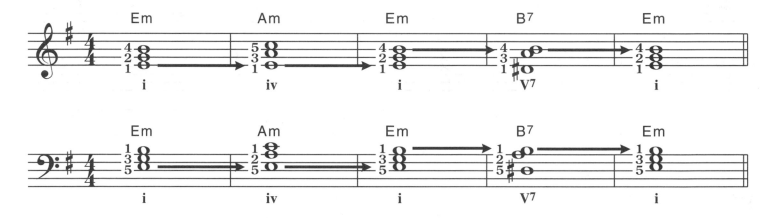

1. Rewrite the above progressions on the following staffs.
2. Add fingering.   3. Add arrows to show the common tones.   4. Play with hands separate.

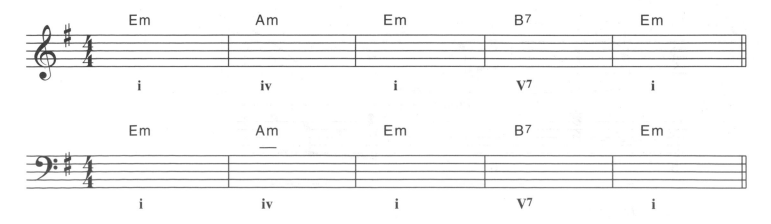

SAKURA

(Cherry Blossoms)

Japanese Folk Song

Andante moderato

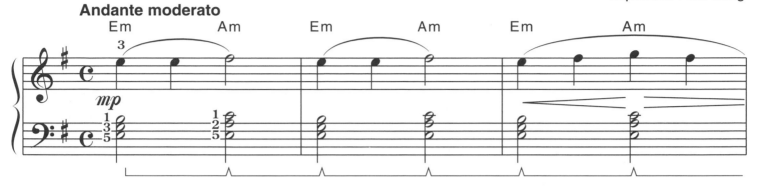

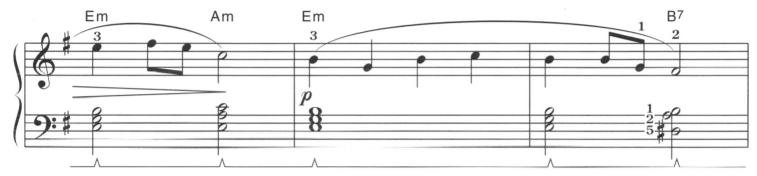

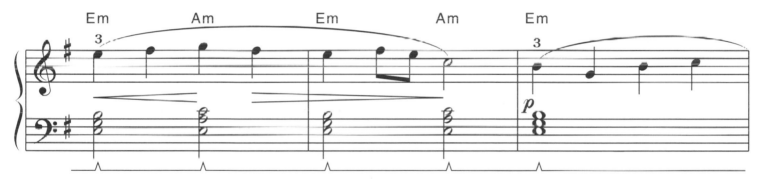

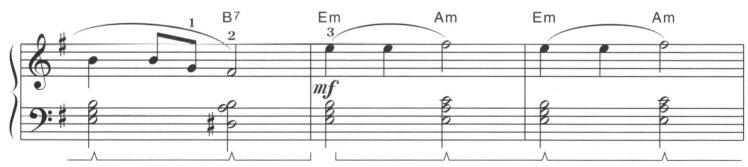

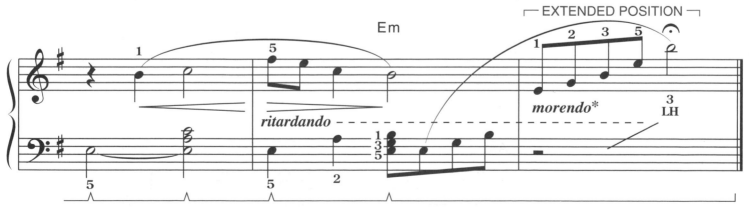

Morendo means *dying away.*

E MINOR PROGRESSION with broken **i**, **iv**, & **V⁷** chords. Play several times with LH.

WAVES OF THE DANUBE

Melodies from *WAVES OF THE DANUBE* were used in the popular hit *"THE ANNIVERSARY SONG."*

KEY OF E MINOR
Key Signature: 1 sharp (F♯)

Moderate waltz tempo

Ivanovici

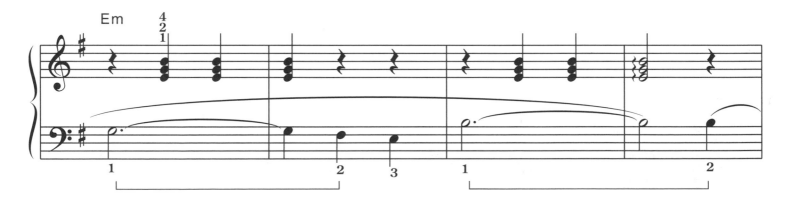

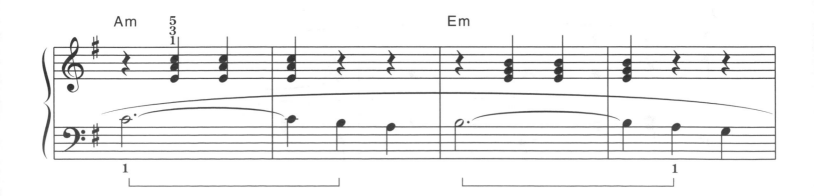

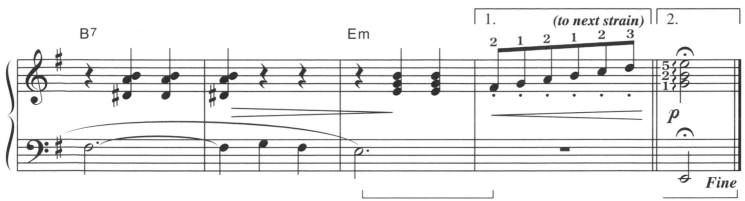

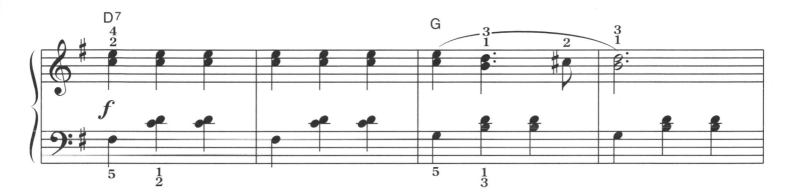

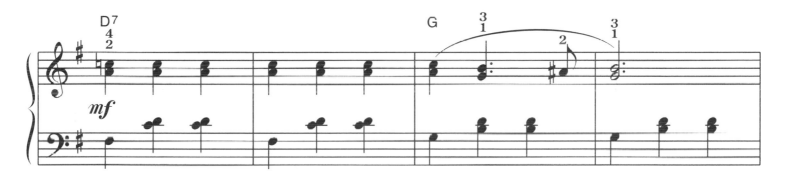

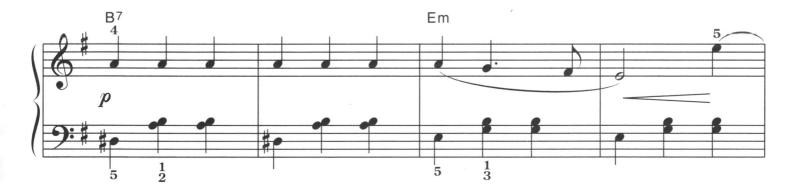

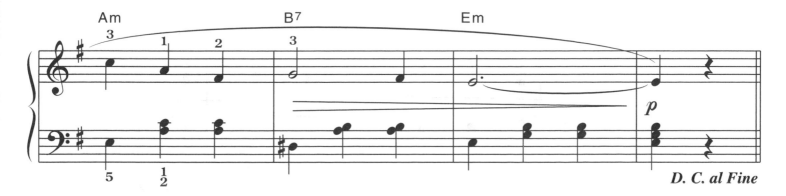

D. C. al Fine

The D Major Scale

Remember that the MAJOR SCALE is made up of two tetrachords *joined* by a whole step.
The second TETRACHORD of the D MAJOR SCALE begins on A.

> There are 2 sharps (F♯ & C♯)
> in the D major scale.

The fingering for the D MAJOR SCALE is the same as for the C MAJOR & G MAJOR scales.

Play slowly and carefully!

KEY OF D MAJOR
Key Signature: 2 sharps (F♯ & C♯)

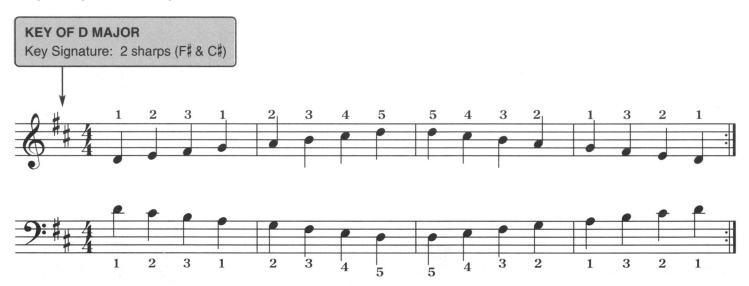

IMPORTANT!   After you have learned the D MAJOR SCALE with hands separate, you may play the hands together in CONTRARY MOTION, as written on the staffs above. Notice that both hands play the same numbered fingers at the same time! Begin with both thumbs on the same D.

Rock-a My Soul 🔊

Spiritual

Allegro moderato

*REMEMBER: Any SHARP sign raises the note one half step. E sharp is the same as F natural!
  Pairs of eighth notes may be played a bit unevenly; long-short.

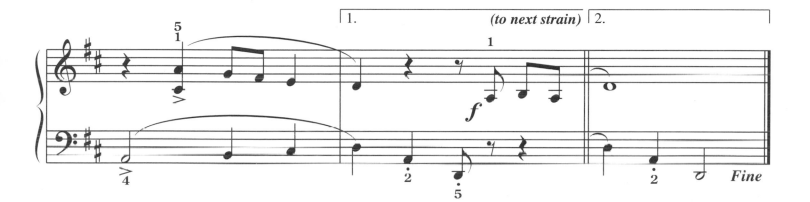

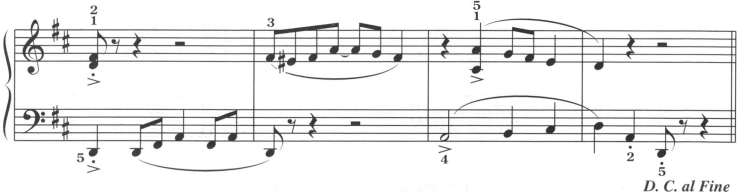

D. C. al Fine

The Key of D Major

1. Write the letter names of the notes of the D MAJOR SCALE, from *left to right,* on the keyboard below. Be sure the WHOLE STEPS & HALF STEPS are correct!

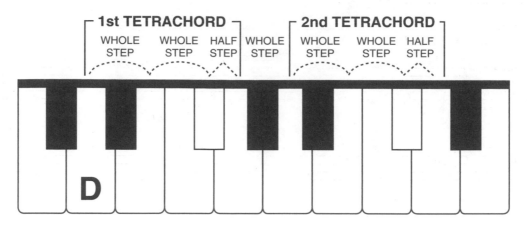

2. Check to be sure you wrote F♯ as the third note of the scale, and C♯ as the seventh note. These notes cannot be called G♭ and D♭, since scale note names must always be in alphabetical order.

3. Complete the tetrachord beginning on D. Write one note over each finger number.

4. Complete the tetrachord beginning on A. Write one note over each finger number.

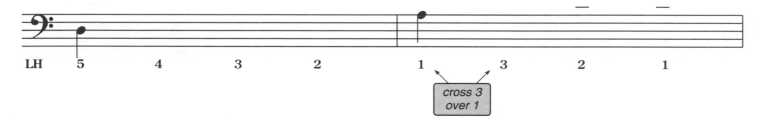

5. Write the fingering UNDER each note of the following LH scale.
6. Play with LH.

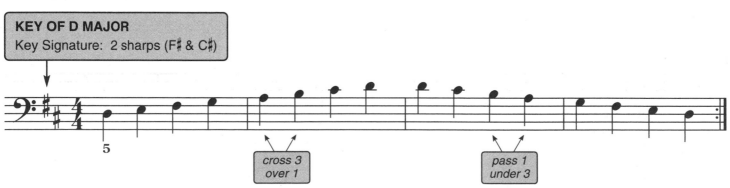

7. Write the fingering OVER each note of the following RH scale.
8. Play with RH.

CALYPSO CARNIVAL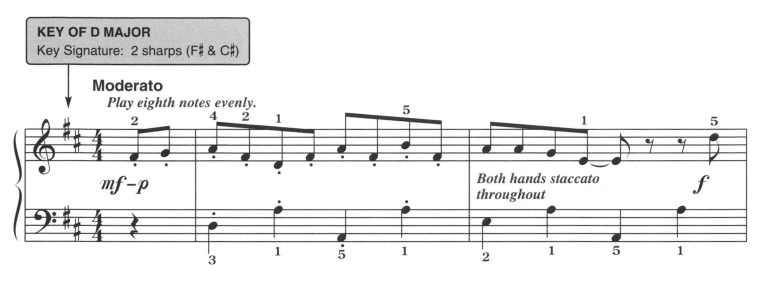

KEY OF D MAJOR
Key Signature: 2 sharps (F♯ & C♯)

Moderato
Play eighth notes evenly.

Both hands staccato throughout

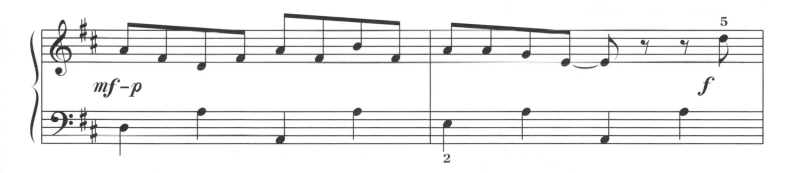

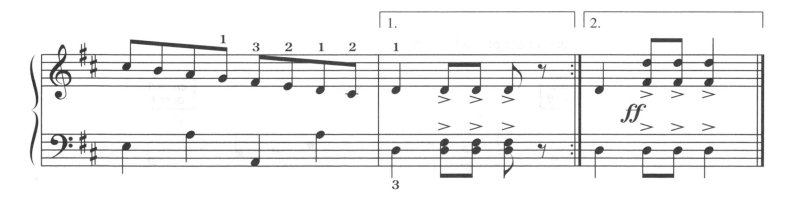

Primary Chords in D Major

Reviewing the D MAJOR SCALE, LH ASCENDING.

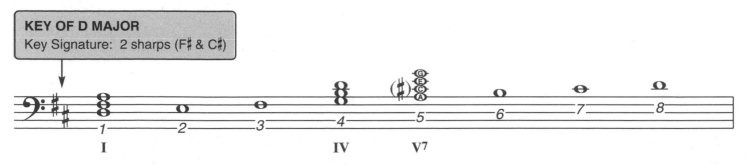

KEY OF D MAJOR
Key Signature: 2 sharps (F♯ & C♯)

The following positions are often used
for smooth progressions:

Primary Chords in D MAJOR

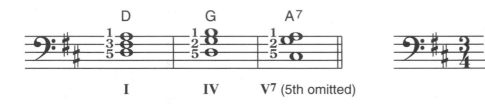

D MAJOR Chord Progression with I, IV, V7 chords.

Play several times, saying the chord names
and numerals aloud:

The same, with chords broken two different ways.
Play several times, saying the chord names and numerals aloud.

YOU'RE IN MY HEART

(Du, du, liegst mir im Herzen)

Allegro moderato

Folk Song

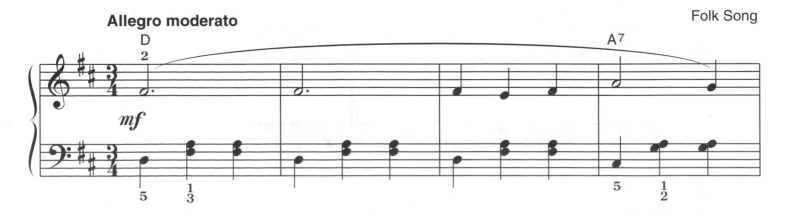

mf

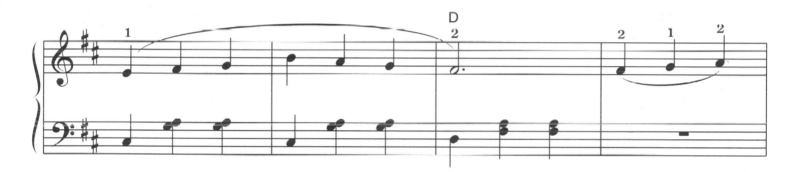

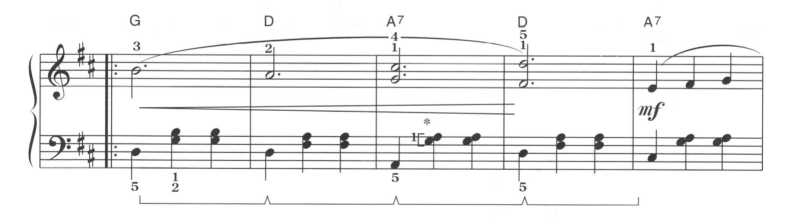

* Play both keys with the side of the thumb.

** *Slide* the thumb from C♯ to D.

Writing the Primary Chords in D Major

KEY OF D MAJOR
Key Signature: 2 sharps (F♯ & C♯)

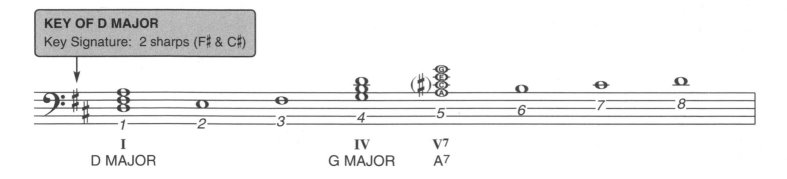

I
D MAJOR

IV
G MAJOR

V⁷
A⁷

The following positions are often used for smooth progressions:

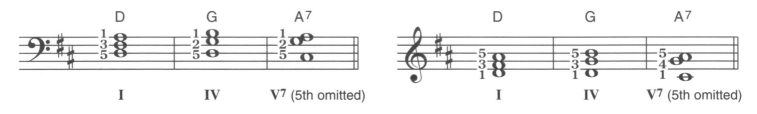

D is the COMMON TONE between **I** & **IV**. **A** is the COMMON TONE between **I** & **V⁷**.

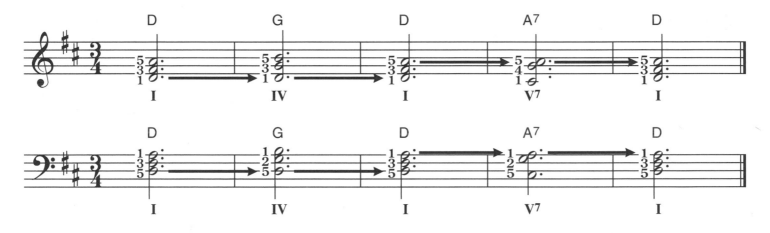

1. Rewrite the above progressions on the following staffs.
2. Add fingering.   3. Add arrows to show the common tones.   4. Play with hands separate.

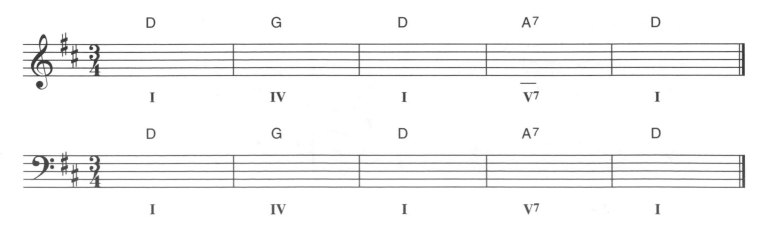

DIVERTIMENTO IN D 🔊

In the Style of Wolfgang Amadeus Mozart

A *DIVERTIMENTO* is a musical "diversion," or recreational piece, usually in classical style. This form was very popular in the eighteenth century. Some of Mozart's pieces using this title have as many as five movements.

Willard A. Palmer

Allegro moderato

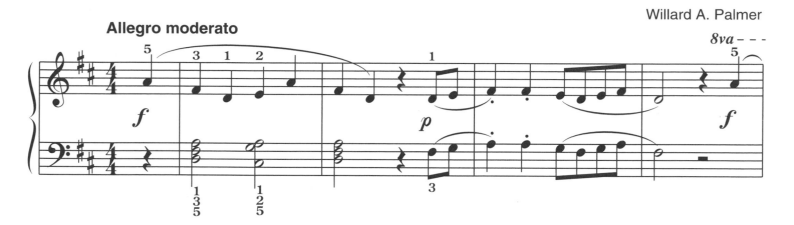

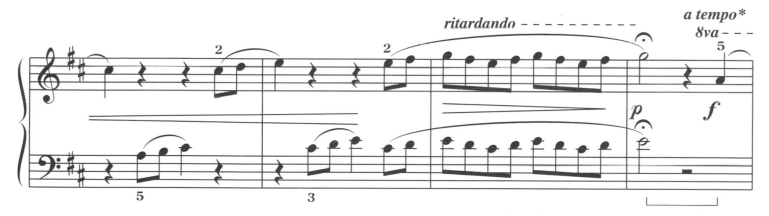

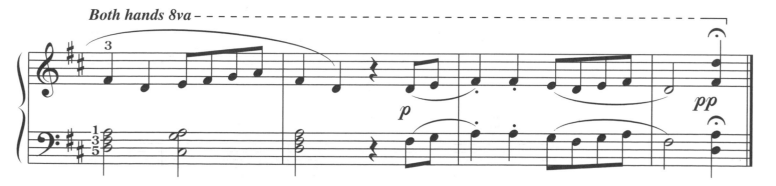

*__a tempo__ = resume the original tempo.

BRAHMS'S LULLABY

Johannes Brahms

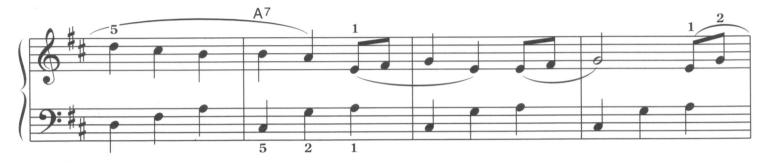

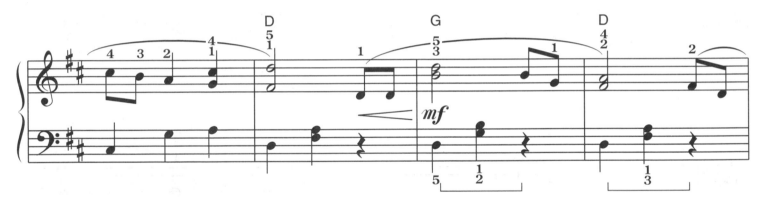

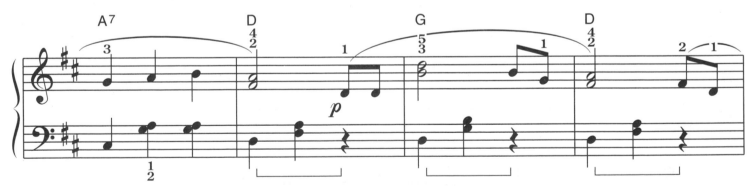

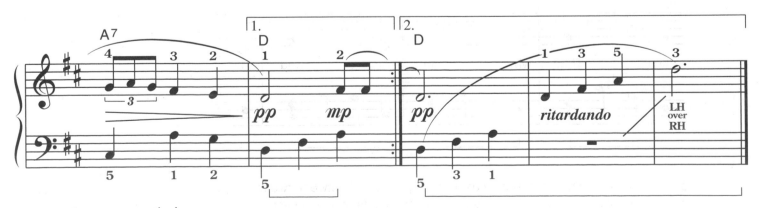

espressivo = expressively

LONESOME ROAD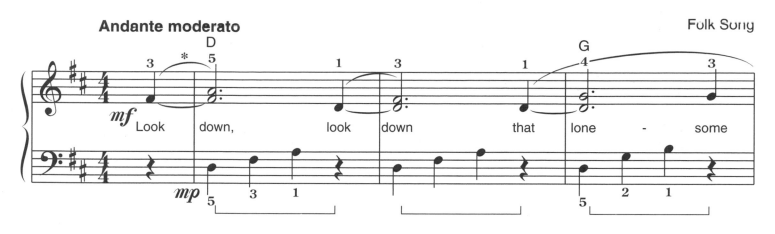

Andante moderato

Folk Song

Look down, look down that lone - some

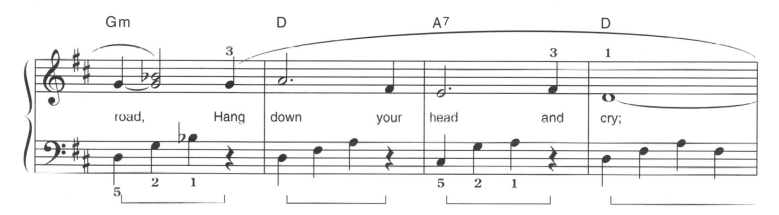

road, Hang down your head and cry;

The best of friends must part some -

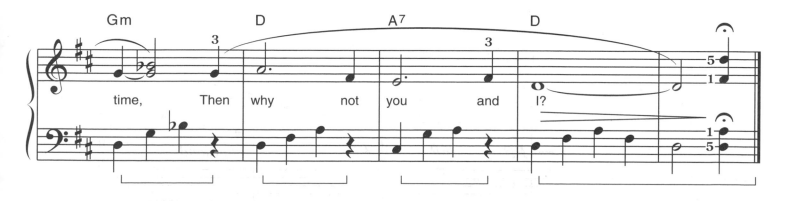

time, Then why not you and I?

*This piece introduces a technic that produces a very legato effect between two melody notes when the second note is part of the same chord. Play the first note and tie it over, holding it as you play the next note.

The Chromatic Scale

The **CHROMATIC SCALE** is made up entirely of **HALF STEPS.**
It goes up and down, using every key, black and white. It may begin on any note.

FINGERING RULES
- Use 3 on each BLACK KEY.
- Use 1 on each white key, except when two white keys are together (no black key between), then use 1-2, or 2-1.

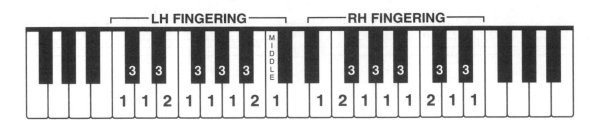

1. Looking at the keyboard above, play the CHROMATIC SCALE with the **LH.** Begin on middle C and GO DOWN one octave.

2. Looking at the keyboard above, play the CHROMATIC SCALE with the **RH.** Begin on E above middle C and GO UP one octave.

Chromatic Warm-Ups

One Octave Chromatic Scale

Play several times daily!

NOTE: It is easy, and fun, to play the CHROMATIC SCALE in CONTRARY MOTION! When the RH begins on E and the LH on C, as above, both hands play the same numbered fingers at the same time.

VILLAGE DANCE

This old folk melody was the inspiration for some of the music of "FIDDLER ON THE ROOF."

Allegro

Folk Tune

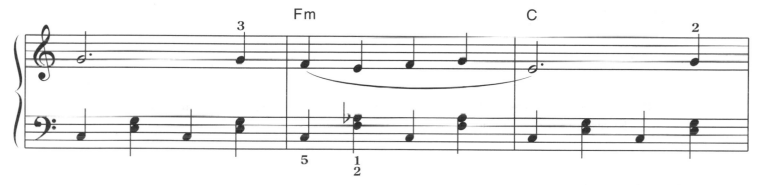

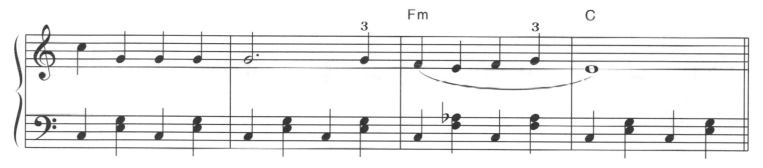

Writing the Chromatic Scale

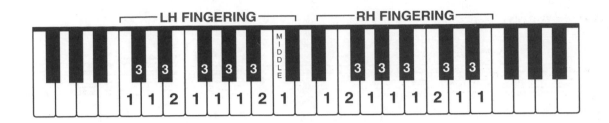

1. Write the chromatic scale, ASCENDING, on the following TREBLE STAFF. (Use half notes.)
   Use SHARPS to indicate BLACK KEYS.

2. Write the chromatic scale, DESCENDING, on the following BASS STAFF.
   Use FLATS to indicate BLACK KEYS.

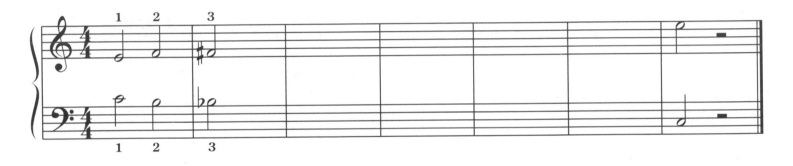

3. Write the chromatic scale, DESCENDING, on the following TREBLE STAFF.
   Use FLATS to indicate BLACK KEYS.

4. Write the chromatic scale, ASCENDING, on the following BASS STAFF.
   Use SHARPS to indicate BLACK KEYS.

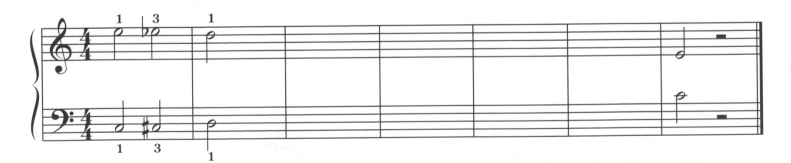

5. Add fingering to the above measures, using the FINGERING RULES at the top of page 60.

6. Play everything on this page, hands separately and together.

CIRCUS MARCH

(Entry of the Gladiators)

Julius Fučik

Moderate march tempo

Triads: The 1st Inversion

ANY ROOT POSITION TRIAD MAY BE INVERTED BY MOVING THE ROOT TO THE TOP.

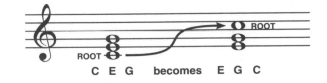

C E G   becomes   E G C

ALL LETTER NAMES ARE THE SAME, BUT THE ROOT IS ON THE TOP.
This is called the FIRST INVERSION.

1st INVERSION TRIADS IN C

Play with RH. Use 1 2 5 on each triad. With the fingers properly spaced for the first triad,
you need only move the hand up ONE WHITE KEY for each of the following triads.

Play the above with LH ONE OCTAVE LOWER. Use 5 3 1 on each triad.

In the 1st inversion, the ROOT
is always the TOP note
of the INTERVAL OF A 4th!   ROOT   This interval is a 4th.
                                                      This interval is a 3rd.

In the following line, each triad is played first in its ROOT POSITION, then in the 1st INVERSION.

The important trick in reading these triads easily is this:

    READ ONLY THE LOWEST NOTE of each triad, then add the upper two notes by INTERVAL!

Play with RH.

THE HOKEY-POKEY 🔊32

All triads down to the first double bar on the next page are 1st inversion triads.
After the double bar, root position triads are also included. READ BY INTERVAL!

Slow swing tempo   Traditional

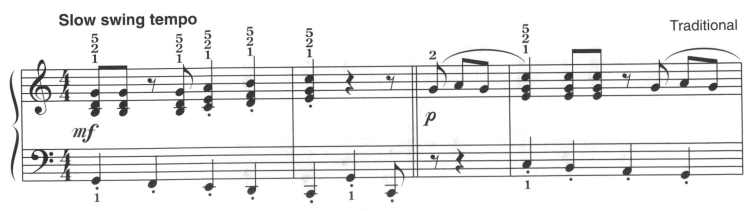

All of the chords in this piece are 1st inversion triads except three.
Find those three and name them before you play.

The eighth notes may be played long-short.

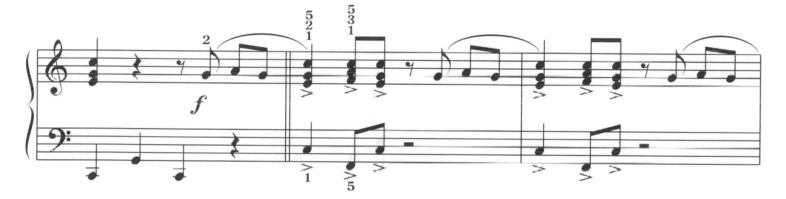

Writing 1st Inversion Triads

**REMEMBER! ANY ROOT POSITION TRIAD MAY BE INVERTED
BY MOVING THE ROOT TO THE TOP.**

C E G   becomes   E G C

**LETTER NAMES ARE THE SAME, BUT THE ROOT IS ON TOP.
THE 3rd OF THE TRIAD IS NOW ON THE BOTTOM!**
This is called the 1st INVERSION.

1. In the measure following each ROOT POSITION triad, write the same triad in the 1st INVERSION.

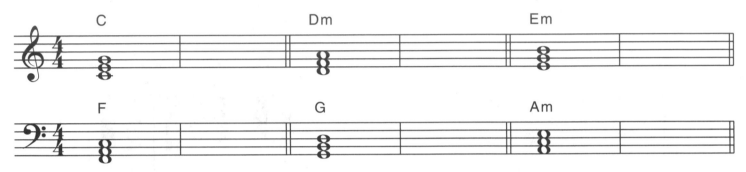

2. Play the TOP LINE above with the RH. Use 1 3 5 on the ROOT POSITION triads.
   Use 1 2 5 on the 1st INVERSION triads.

3. Play the BOTTOM LINE above with the LH. Use 5 3 1 on the ROOT POSITION triads.
   Use 5 3 1 also on the 1st INVERSION triads.

Triads in the 1st INVERSION look like this:

**When a triad has this appearance, the note at
the TOP of the interval of a 4th is the ROOT!**

4. Draw an arrow (←) pointing to the ROOT of each triad in No. 1, above.

CHORALE 🔊

5. Using the notes given below as ROOTS, add two notes below each to make 1st INVERSION triads.
6. Play. Use RH 1 2 5 on the notes in treble clef. Use LH 5 3 1 on the notes in bass clef.

Adagio

Invert the Triads!

Each triad in the left column is in ROOT POSITION.

1. Write the letter names on each keyboard in the right column, showing the same triad in the 1st INVERSION.

2. Draw arrows pointing UP to the ROOT of *each* root position and 1st inversion triad.
    The first pair of triads is completed for you, as an example.

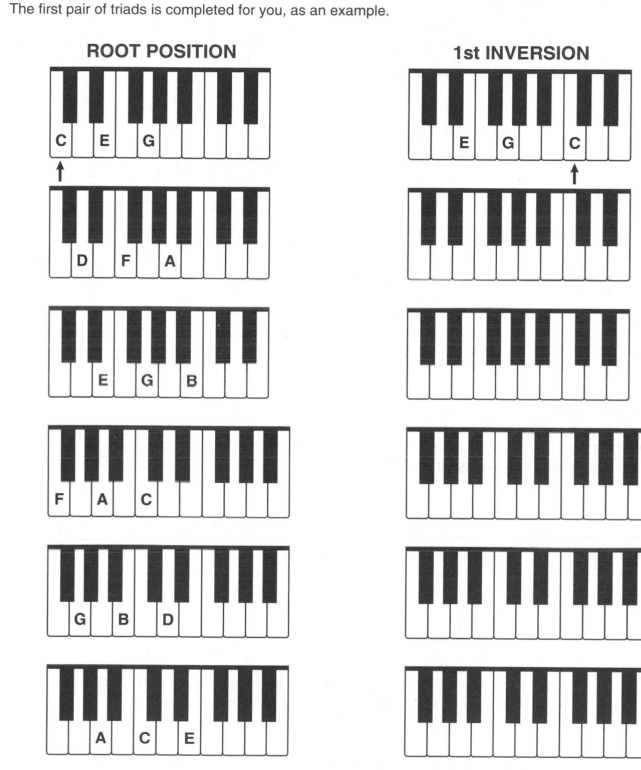

3. BONUS QUESTION: When a triad is in the 1st INVERSION, which note is on the BOTTOM?

    ANSWER: ROOT   THIRD   FIFTH   (Circle the right answer.)

    Score 10 for each correct 1st INVERSION TRIAD. _____
    Score 2 for each correct ARROW. _____
    Score 30 for BONUS QUESTION. _____
    PERFECT SCORE = 100.   **YOUR SCORE:** _____

NIGHT SONG

A "Night Song" could also be called a NOCTURNE or a SERENADE.

This piece is much easier than it looks or sounds, because every 3-note chord, including the broken chords in the beginning of the RH, is a 1st inversion triad. They are all fingered 1 2 5 in the RH, or 5 3 1 in the LH.

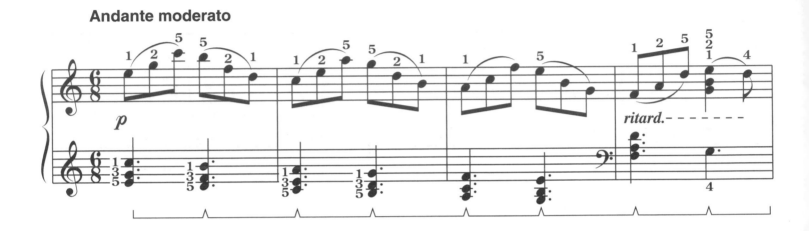

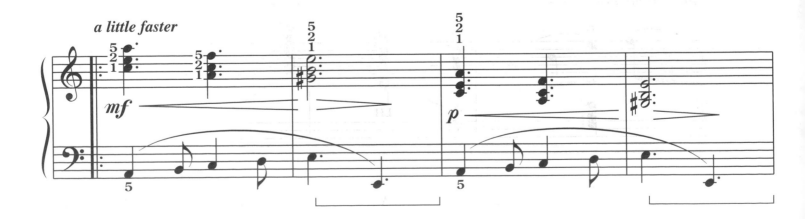

a little slower

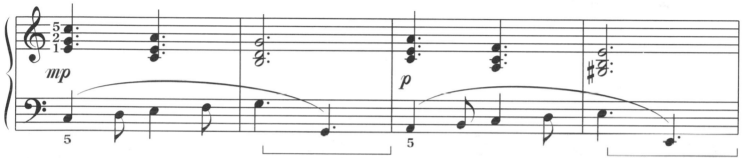

After repeating, D. C. al ⊕, then CODA
(Repeat from the beginning to the sign ⊕,
then skip to the CODA.)

⊕ **CODA** (an added ending)
molto ritardando -

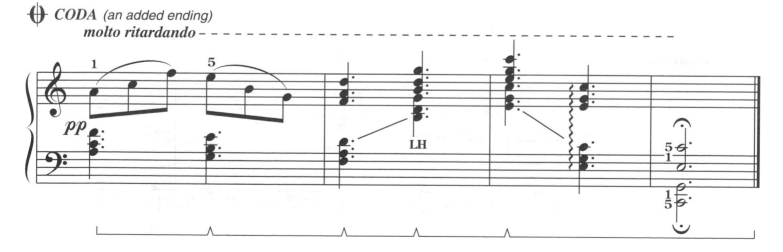

HAVA NAGILA

"Come, sweetheart, and dance with me. It is the final day of harvest, and we must leave our cares behind us."
This is probably the most popular of all Israeli folk songs.

Traditional

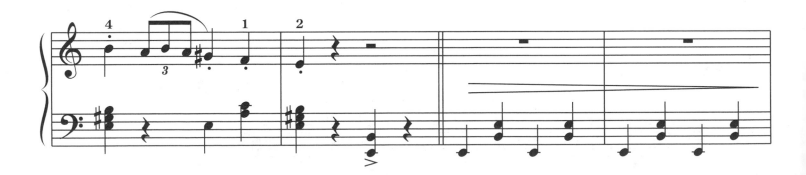

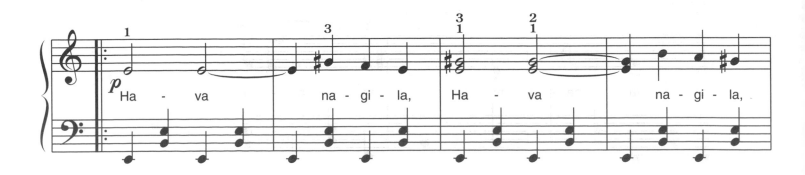

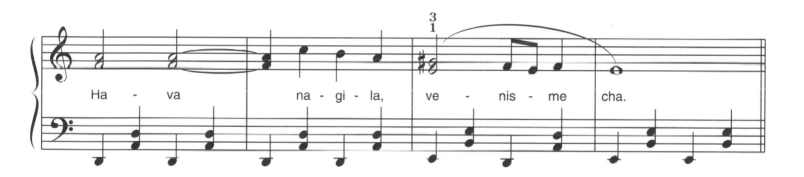

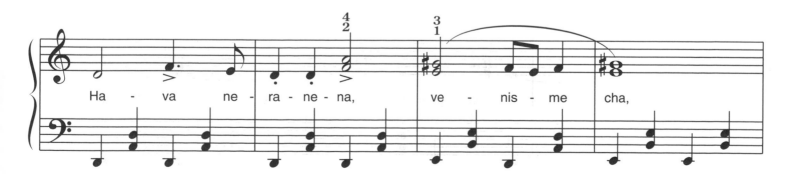

Ha - va ne - ra - ne - na, Ha - va ne -

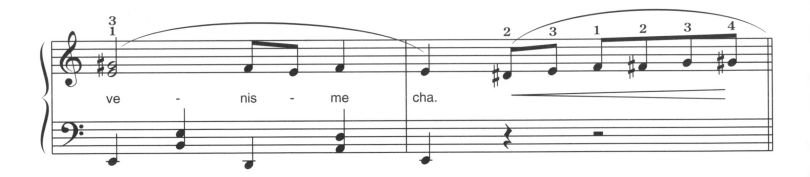

ra - ne - na, Ha - va ne - ra - ne - na,

ve - nis - me cha.

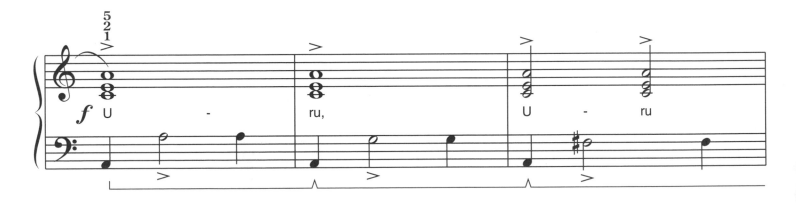

U - ru, U - ru

a - chim, U - ru a - chim, b' - lev sa - me - ach

(staccato)

U - ru a - chim, b' - lev sa - me - ach U - ru a - chim, b' -

accelerando poco a poco

lev sa - me - ach U - ru a - chim, b' - lev sa - me - ach

U - ru a - chim, U - ru a - chim, b' - lev sa - me -

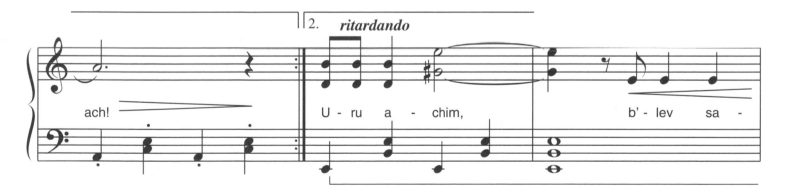

ach! U - ru a - chim, b' - lev sa -

ritardando

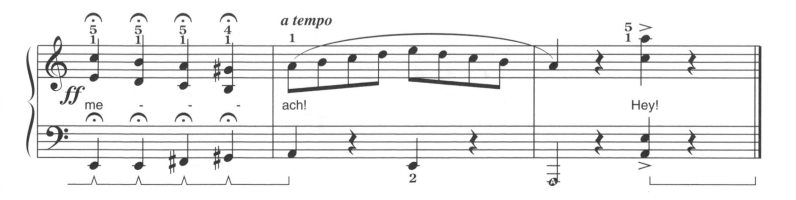

a tempo

ff me - - - ach! Hey!

Triads: The 2nd Inversion

ANY 1st INVERSION TRIAD MAY BE INVERTED AGAIN BY MOVING THE LOWEST NOTE TO THE TOP.

ALL LETTER NAMES ARE THE SAME, BUT THE ROOT IS IN THE MIDDLE.
This is called the SECOND INVERSION.

2nd INVERSION TRIADS IN C

Play with LH. Use 5 2 1 on each triad. With the fingers properly spaced for the first triad, you need only move the hand up ONE WHITE KEY for each of the following triads.

Play the above with RH ONE OCTAVE HIGHER. Use 1 3 5 on each triad.

In the 2nd inversion, the ROOT is always the TOP note of the INTERVAL OF A 4th!

This interval is a 3rd.
This interval is a 4th.

In the following line, each ROOT POSITION triad is followed by the same triad in the 1st INVERSION, then in the 2nd INVERSION. Read only the bottom note of each triad, and add the remaining notes by INTERVAL!

Play with RH.

REMEMBER: If the root is on the *bottom*, the triad is in **ROOT POSITION.**
If the root is on the *top*, the triad is in the **1st INVERSION.**
If the root is in the *middle*, the triad is in the **2nd INVERSION.**

Play the last line of music above with the RH, saying
"ROOT POSITION, 1st INVERSION, 2nd INVERSION," etc., as you play.

SPACE SHUTTLE BLUES 🔊

Play the LH alone first, naming the root of each triad.
Every LH chord is a 2nd inversion triad, so the root is always the MIDDLE note!

Moderate blues tempo

I'm gon-na build my-self a shut-tle; I'm gon-na take off to the

moon! I'm gon-na build my-self a shut-tle;

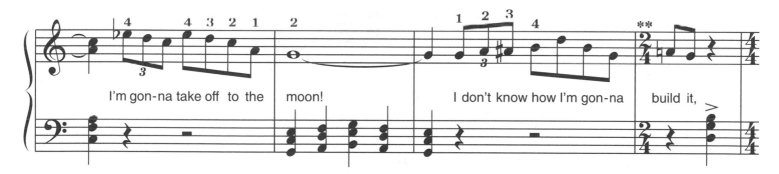

I'm gon-na take off to the moon! I don't know how I'm gon-na build it,

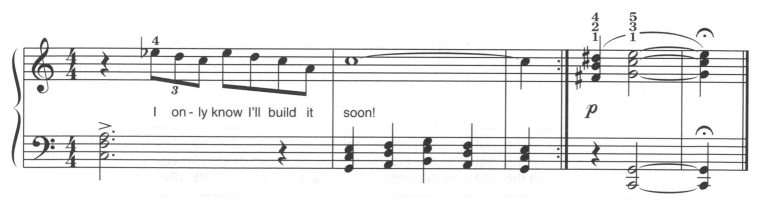

I on-ly know I'll build it soon!

* Play the pairs of eighth notes a bit unevenly, long-short.

** Notice that the time signature changes for one measure only.
In this new time signature: 2 means **2 beats** to each measure.
4 means a **quarter note** gets one beat.

OLYMPIC PROCESSION

Each LH chord in this piece, and every RH 3-note chord, is a 2nd inversion triad!

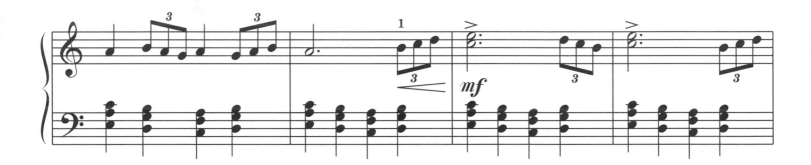

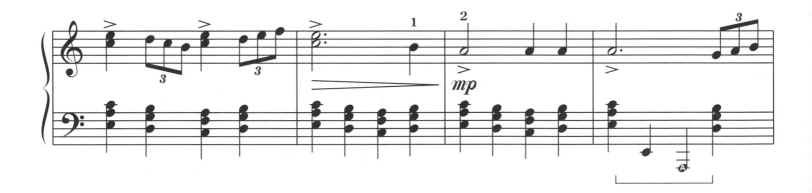

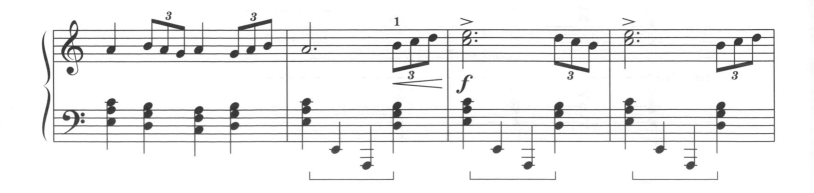

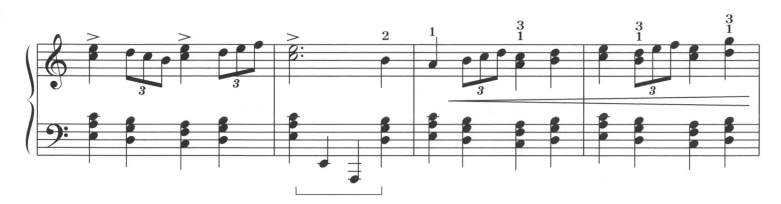

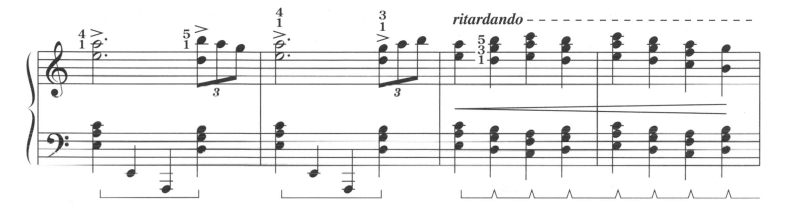

Maestoso *(majestically)*

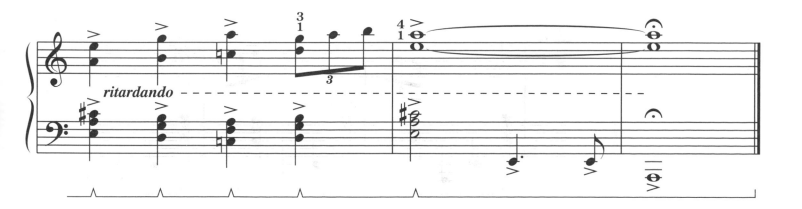

Writing 2nd Inversion Triads

**REMEMBER! ANY 1st INVERSION TRIAD MAY BE INVERTED AGAIN
BY MOVING THE LOWEST NOTE TO THE TOP.**

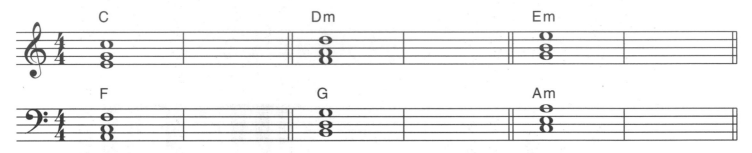

E G C   becomes   G C E

**LETTER NAMES ARE THE SAME, BUT THE ROOT IS IN THE MIDDLE.
THE 5th OF THE TRIAD IS NOW ON THE BOTTOM!
This is called the 2nd INVERSION.**

1. In the measure following each 1st inversion triad, write the same triad in the 2nd INVERSION.

2. Play the TOP LINE above with the RH. Use 1 2 5 on the 1st INVERSION triads.
    Use 1 3 5 on the 2nd INVERSION triads.

3. Play the BOTTOM LINE above with the LH. Use 5 3 1 on the 1st INVERSION triads.
    Use 5 2 1 on the 2nd INVERSION triads.

Triads in the 2nd INVERSION look like this:

**When a triad has this appearance, the note at
the TOP of the interval of a 4th is the ROOT!**

ROOT ➡

INTERVAL OF A 3rd
INTERVAL OF A 4th

4. Draw an arrow (←) pointing to the ROOT of each triad in No. 1, above.

CHORALE 🔊36

Andante moderato

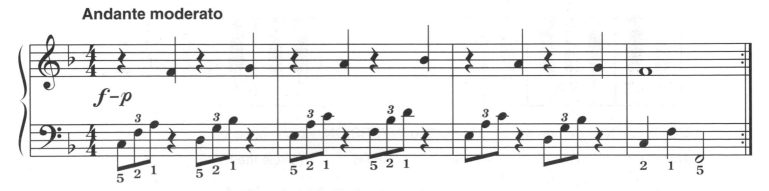

5. Using the notes given in the TREBLE CLEF above as ROOTS, add a note above and a note below each
    to make 2nd INVERSION TRIADS. (Add notes only in the UPPER STAFF.)

6. Play. Use 1 3 5 on each RH triad.

Invert the Inversions!

Each triad in the left column is in the 1st INVERSION.

1. Write the letter names on each keyboard in the right column,
   showing the same triad in the 2nd INVERSION.

2. Draw arrows pointing UP to the ROOT of *each* 1st and 2nd INVERSION triad.
   The first pair of triads is completed for you, as an example.

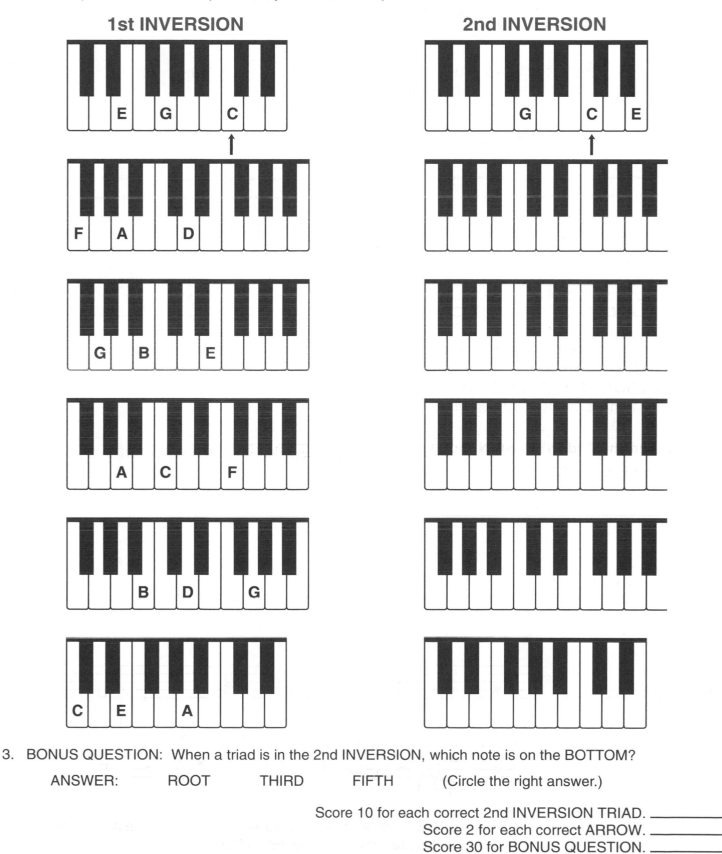

1st INVERSION

2nd INVERSION

3. BONUS QUESTION: When a triad is in the 2nd INVERSION, which note is on the BOTTOM?

      ANSWER: ROOT   THIRD   FIFTH   (Circle the right answer.)

Score 10 for each correct 2nd INVERSION TRIAD. _____

Score 2 for each correct ARROW. _____

Score 30 for BONUS QUESTION. _____

PERFECT SCORE = 100.   **YOUR SCORE:** _____

Triads in All Positions

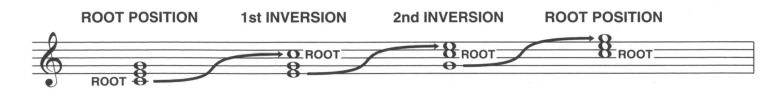

ROOT POSITION   **1st INVERSION**   **2nd INVERSION**   **ROOT POSITION**

PLAY THE FOLLOWING:

C MAJOR TRIAD

G MAJOR TRIAD

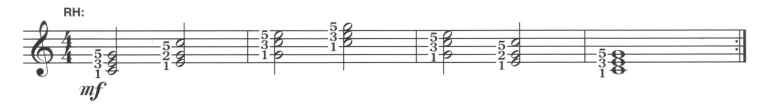

The same, beginning one octave higher:

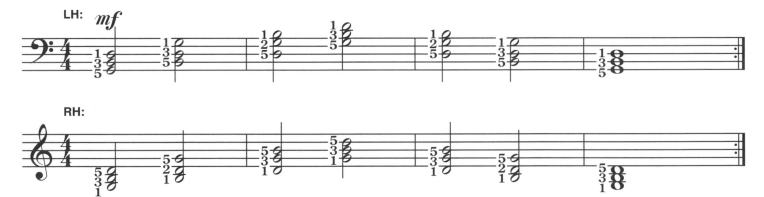

IMPORTANT!

Repeat all of the above, using ARPEGGIATED CHORDS:  *etc.*

FAREWELL TO THEE (ALOHA OE)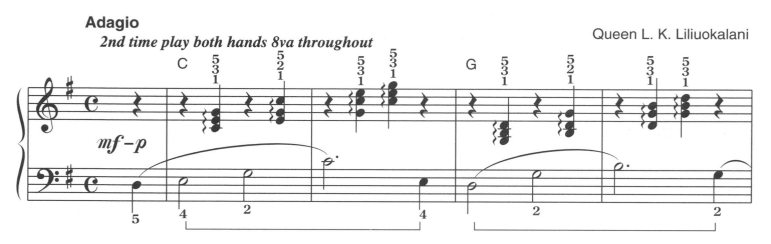

"Aloha Oe" is used in the Hawaiian Islands as a greeting or farewell. This well-known song, which is played and sung for tourists arriving and leaving the islands, was composed by the last queen of the Hawaiian Islands, Lydia Kamekaha Liliuokalani, who reigned in 1891–93.

Adagio
2nd time play both hands 8va throughout

Queen L. K. Liliuokalani

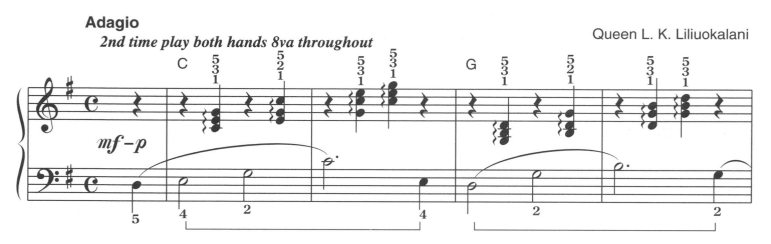

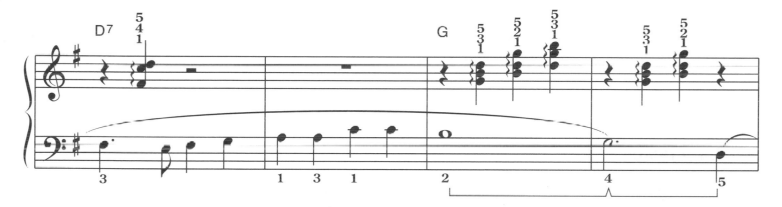

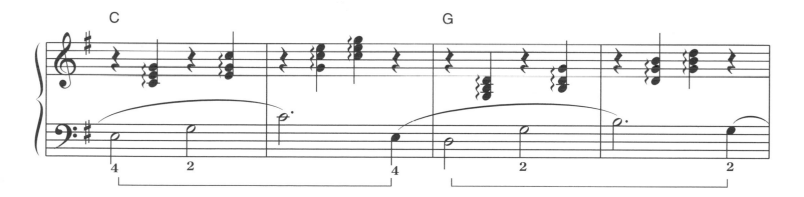

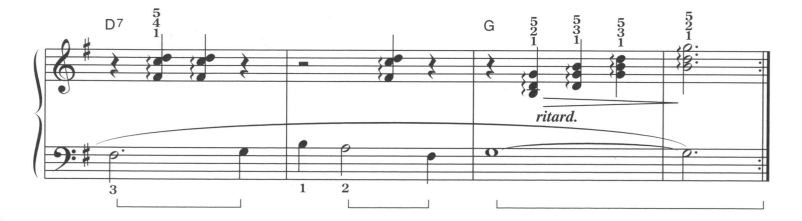

BLACK FOREST POLKA 🔊

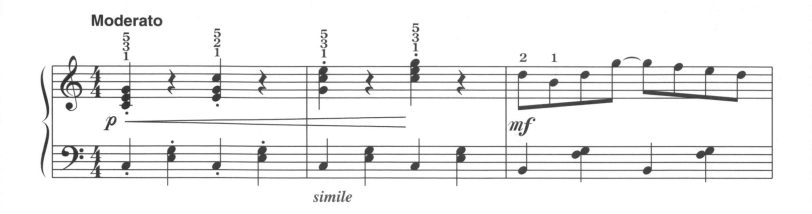

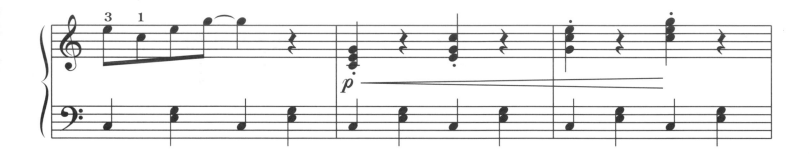

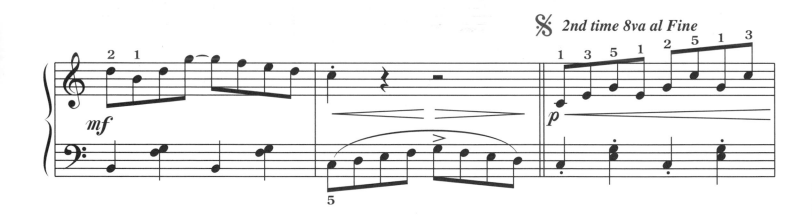

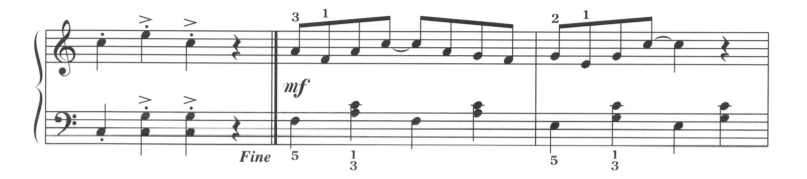

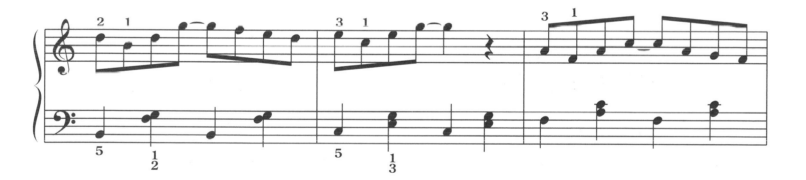

D. S. ℅ al Fine*

* *D. S. (Dal Segno)* means *from the sign.*

D. S. ℅ al Fine means *repeat from the sign ℅ and play to the Fine.*

Writing Triads in All Positions

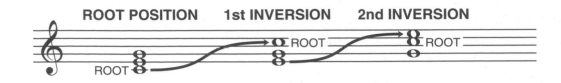

1. In the measure after each ROOT POSITION triad, write the same triad in the 1st INVERSION.
   In the next measure, write the same triad in the 2nd INVERSION.

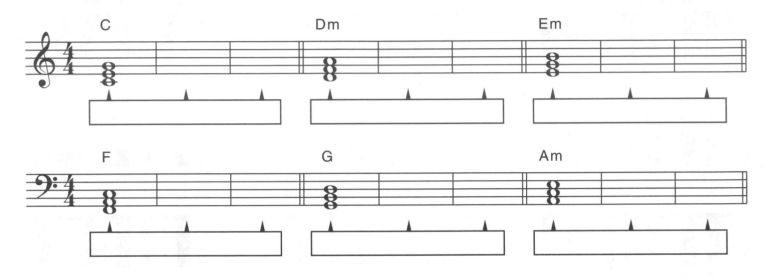

Review—Major & Minor Triads

MAJOR TRIADS in ROOT POSITION consist of a ROOT, a MAJOR 3rd (4 half steps above the root) and a PERFECT 5th (7 half steps above the root).

MINOR TRIADS in ROOT POSITION consist of a ROOT, a MINOR 3rd (3 half steps above the root) and a PERFECT 5th (7 half steps above the root).

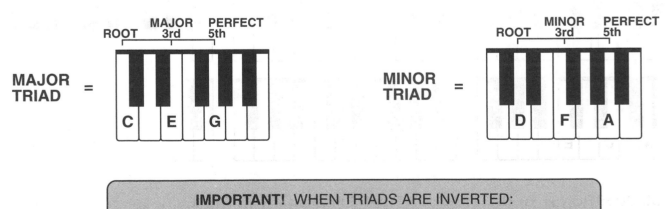

IMPORTANT! WHEN TRIADS ARE INVERTED:
MAJOR TRIADS REMAIN MAJOR; MINOR TRIADS REMAIN MINOR.

2. In No. 1 above, write "MAJOR TRIADS" or "MINOR TRIADS" in the boxes below each group of 3 triads.

3. Play the TOP LINE of No. 1 with the RH.

4. Play the BOTTOM LINE of No. 1 with the LH.

Inverting Major & Minor Triads

Each triad in the left column is in ROOT POSITION.
The TOP 3 triads are MAJOR TRIADS. The bottom 3 are MINOR TRIADS.

1. Write the letter names on each keyboard in the middle column,
   showing the same triads in the 1st INVERSION.

2. Write the letter names on each keyboard in the right column,
   showing the same triads in the 2nd INVERSION.

3. Draw arrows pointing UP to the ROOT of each triad.

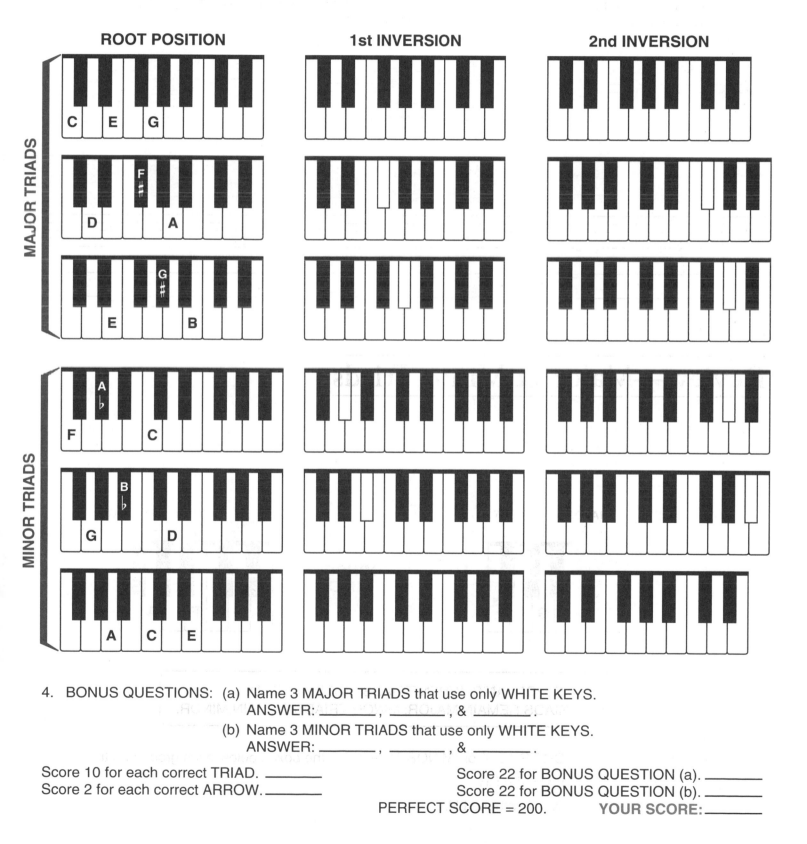

4. BONUS QUESTIONS: (a) Name 3 MAJOR TRIADS that use only WHITE KEYS.
   ANSWER: _____ , _____ , & _____ .
   (b) Name 3 MINOR TRIADS that use only WHITE KEYS.
   ANSWER: _____ , _____ , & _____ .

Score 10 for each correct TRIAD. _____   Score 22 for BONUS QUESTION (a). _____
Score 2 for each correct ARROW. _____   Score 22 for BONUS QUESTION (b). _____
PERFECT SCORE = 200.   YOUR SCORE: _____

Two-Part Writing

In some music, one hand must play two melodies that have notes of different time values, at the same time.

1st or principal part (the melody). Play with RH.

2nd part (counter-melody). Play with RH.

When both parts are written on ONE staff, the note-stems of the UPPER melody are turned UP, and the note-stems of the LOWER melody are turned DOWN. This is called TWO-PART WRITING.
Play with RH.

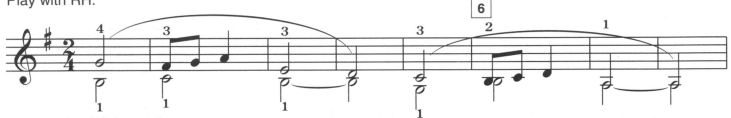

In the 6th measure, the upper (1st) part begins with the eighth note B. The lower (2nd) part has the same B, but it is a half note. Play the B only once, and hold it for the value of the half note while the upper melody continues.

In the 7th and 8th measures, both parts are the same. In this case, the note is given two stems, but it is played only once.

Processional from
POMP AND CIRCUMSTANCE NO. 1

This is one of the most famous of all melodies. It is often played for royal coronation celebrations and graduation ceremonies.

Sir Edward Elgar

Molto maestoso*

* *Molto* means *very*.   *Molto maestoso* means *very majestically*.

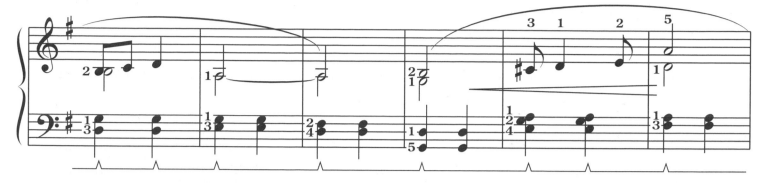

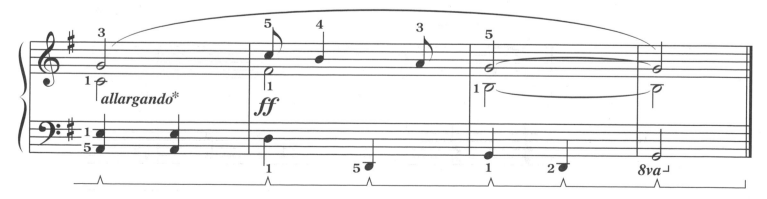

* *Allargando* means *broadening.* It means an increased dignity of style,
slowing the tempo while maintaining or increasing volume.

Writing in Two Parts

Sometimes two melodies with different time values must be written on the same staff.

The UPPER melody (usually called the principal melody) is written with the stems UP.
The LOWER melody (usually called the counter-melody) is written with the stems DOWN.

This is called TWO-PART WRITING. When both melodies have the same note, the stems must point in both directions.

1. PLAY WITH TWO HANDS. Play notes with stems UP with the RH.
    Play notes with stems DOWN with the LH.

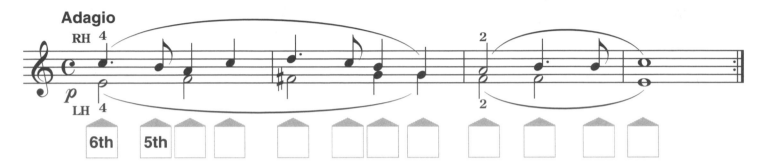

2. In the boxes above, write the name of each HARMONIC INTERVAL produced by the two parts, as shown in the first two examples. (The 5th is an interval because the E is held for two beats.) When both parts have the same note, write S (same).

If the LH has to play something else, the RH may be required to play two parts in the treble clef. In the music below, the two parts can easily be played with the RH by using the THUMB on the LOWER NOTES.

3. PLAY WITH RH ONLY.

In the following example, two more parts have been added for the LH.

4. PLAY WITH BOTH HANDS. Play the two upper parts with the RH.
    Play the two lower parts with the LH.

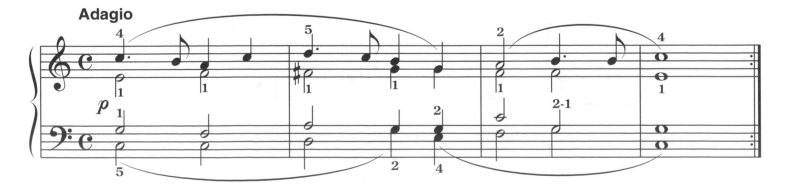

DARK EYES

Adagio, freely

Russian Folk Song

ETUDE, OPUS 10, NO. 3
(Theme)

Frédéric Chopin

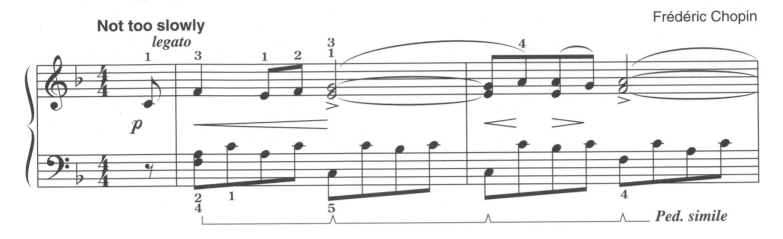

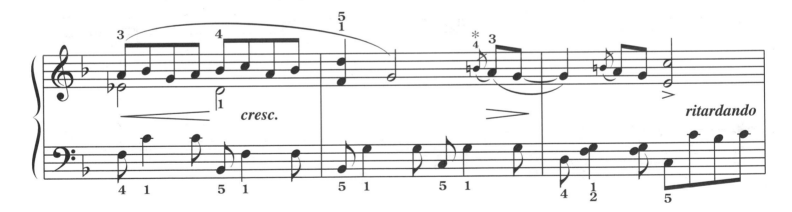

* ♪ = grace note. It is a note played very quickly, almost together with the following large note.

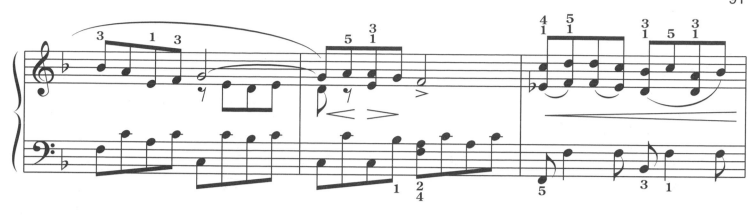

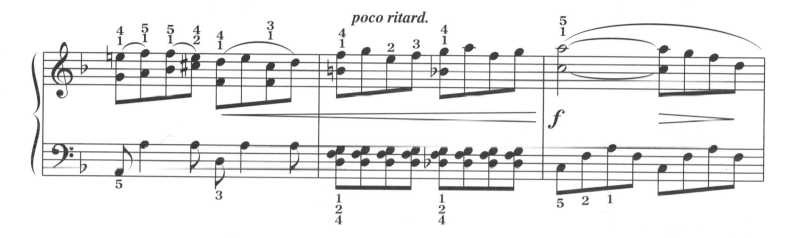

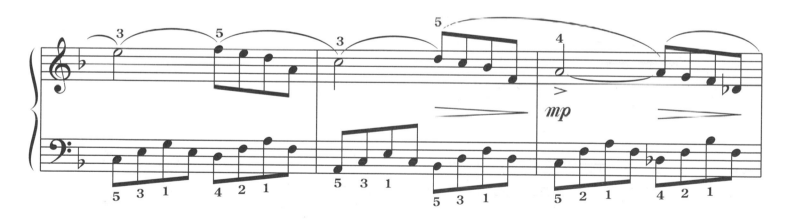

THE COMPLETE
"7th CHORD VOCABULARY"

Play each of the following 7th chords.
Stems up = RH.   Stems down = LH.

Say the note names as you play.

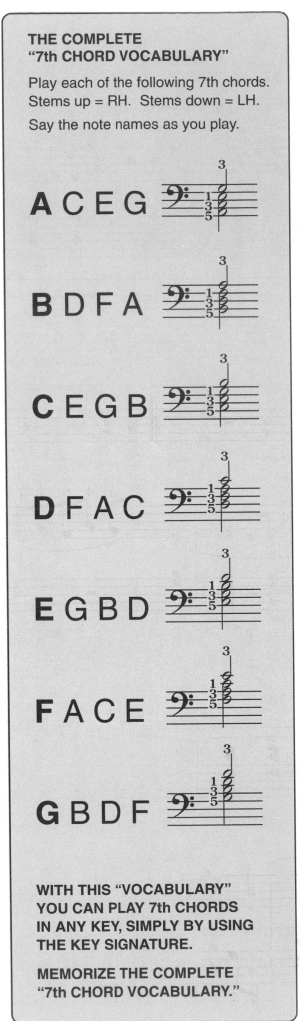

A C E G

B D F A

C E G B

D F A C

E G B D

F A C E

G B D F

WITH THIS "VOCABULARY"
YOU CAN PLAY 7th CHORDS
IN ANY KEY, SIMPLY BY USING
THE KEY SIGNATURE.

MEMORIZE THE COMPLETE
"7th CHORD VOCABULARY."

Seventh Chord Review

A **SEVENTH CHORD** MAY BE FORMED
BY ADDING TO THE **ROOT POSITION TRIAD**
A NOTE THAT IS A **SEVENTH** ABOVE THE ROOT.

THE FOUR NOTES OF A SEVENTH CHORD ARE:

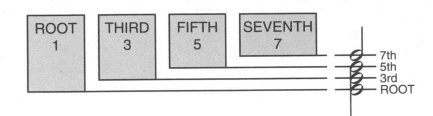

SEVENTH CHORDS IN **ROOT POSITION**
(WITH ROOT AT THE BOTTOM)
LOOK LIKE THIS:

The 5th is often omitted from the seventh chord.
This makes it simple to play with one hand.
PLAY WITH LH.

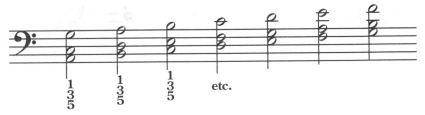

The 3rd is sometimes omitted.
PLAY WITH LH.

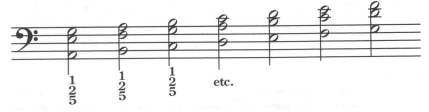

All seventh chords on this page are in **ROOT POSITION!**

REMEMBER: When the interval from the lowest note
of the chord to the highest is a 7th,
the BOTTOM NOTE is the ROOT!

SWINGING SEVENTHS

Every LH chord in this piece is a seventh chord in root position! Play the LH alone at first.
Notice which seventh chords have the 5th omitted and which have the 3rd omitted.

Moderately slow, with a "swing feeling"

D. C. al 𝄋, then CODA

𝄋 CODA

morendo - - - - - - - - - e - - - - - - - -ritardando - - - - - -

Writing Seventh Chords

A SEVENTH CHORD has 4 notes, a series of 3rds stacked one above the other:

A SEVENTH CHORD may be built by adding a 3rd above any root position triad:

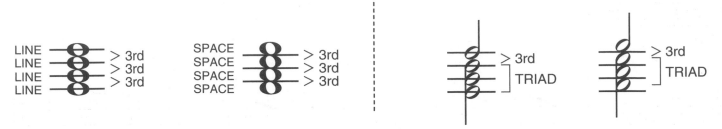

It is best to consider the SEVENTH CHORD as a TRIAD (root, 3rd, 5th) with the added note a 7th ABOVE THE ROOT, since that is the reason it is called a seventh chord.

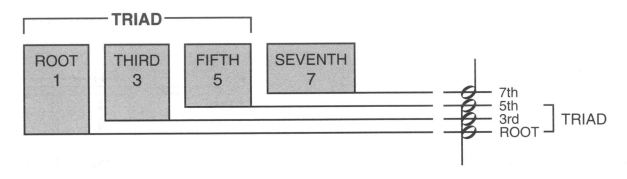

The "7th Chord Vocabulary"

When seventh CHORDS are spelled in ROOT POSITION, always skip ONE LETTER of the MUSICAL ALPHABET between each note. This gives you the following basic **7th CHORD VOCABULARY:**

A C E G   B D F A   C E G B   D F A C   E G B D   F A C E   G B D F

The sharps or flats included in the seventh chords spelled with these letters will depend on the key signature of the music you are playing.

1. Complete each column by adding the note-names of the 3rd, 5th & 7th above each given root, as shown in the first column.
2. Play each of these basic seventh chords, using RH 1 2 3 5. Play them again, using LH 5 3 2 1.

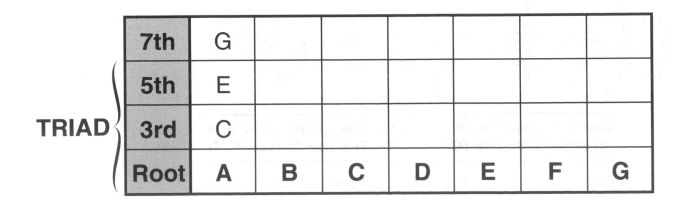

	7th	G						
	5th	E						
TRIAD	3rd	C						
	Root	A	B	C	D	E	F	G

V⁷ Chords in All Positions

The **V⁷ CHORD** is built on the 5th note of the scale.
The **V⁷ CHORD** is formed from a MAJOR TRIAD with a note added that is a 7th above the ROOT.
The **V⁷ CHORD** may be played in the following positions.

KEY OF C MAJOR

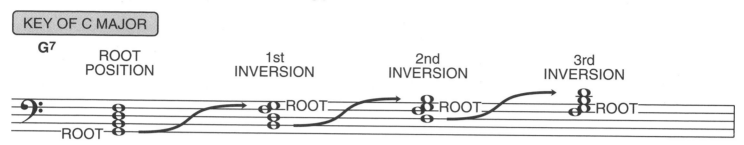

The 5th is *often* omitted from the **V⁷** chord. The 3rd is *sometimes* omitted instead.
When a note is omitted from the chord, it will have only three positions.

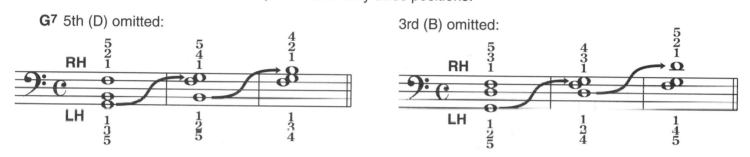

1. Play the above G⁷ CHORDS, first with the LH, as written, then with the RH, one octave higher than written.

The **V⁷** CHORDS in the following examples are given in the ROOT POSITIONS.

2. In the two measures following each chord below, write the two inversions of the chord.
3. Play, first with LH, as written, then with RH, one octave higher.

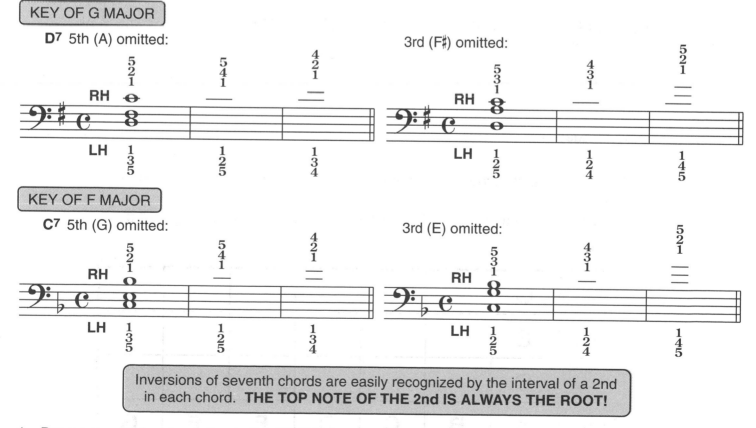

4. Draw an arrow (←) pointing to the ROOT of each V⁷ chord above.

Theme from
THE POLOVETSIAN DANCES

This melody from Borodin's opera "Prince Igor" was used in the 1953 Broadway musical "Kismet,"
as the basis for the very popular song, "Stranger in Paradise."

See if you can identify all the seventh chords.

A. Borodin

Eighth notes should be played evenly!

*OPTIONAL: Roll each LH chord. Pedal as you wish.

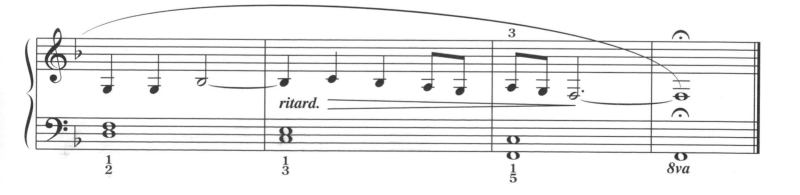

Sixteenth Notes

When one sixteenth note is written alone, it looks like this:

Sixteenth notes are usually in **pairs** or **groups of four,** written like this:

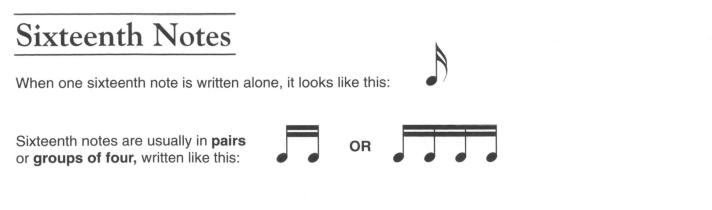

OR

Four sixteenth notes are played in the time of **one quarter note.**

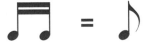

COUNT: 1 - a - & - a
or 4   six-teenth notes

There can be 16 sixteenth notes in one measure of **COMMON** ($\frac{4}{4}$) **TIME!**

Play several times: first ADAGIO, then ANDANTE, then ALLEGRO MODERATO.

Two sixteenth notes are played in the time of **one eighth note.**

Play several times: first ADAGIO, then ANDANTE, then ALLEGRO MODERATO.

Writing and Counting Sixteenth Notes

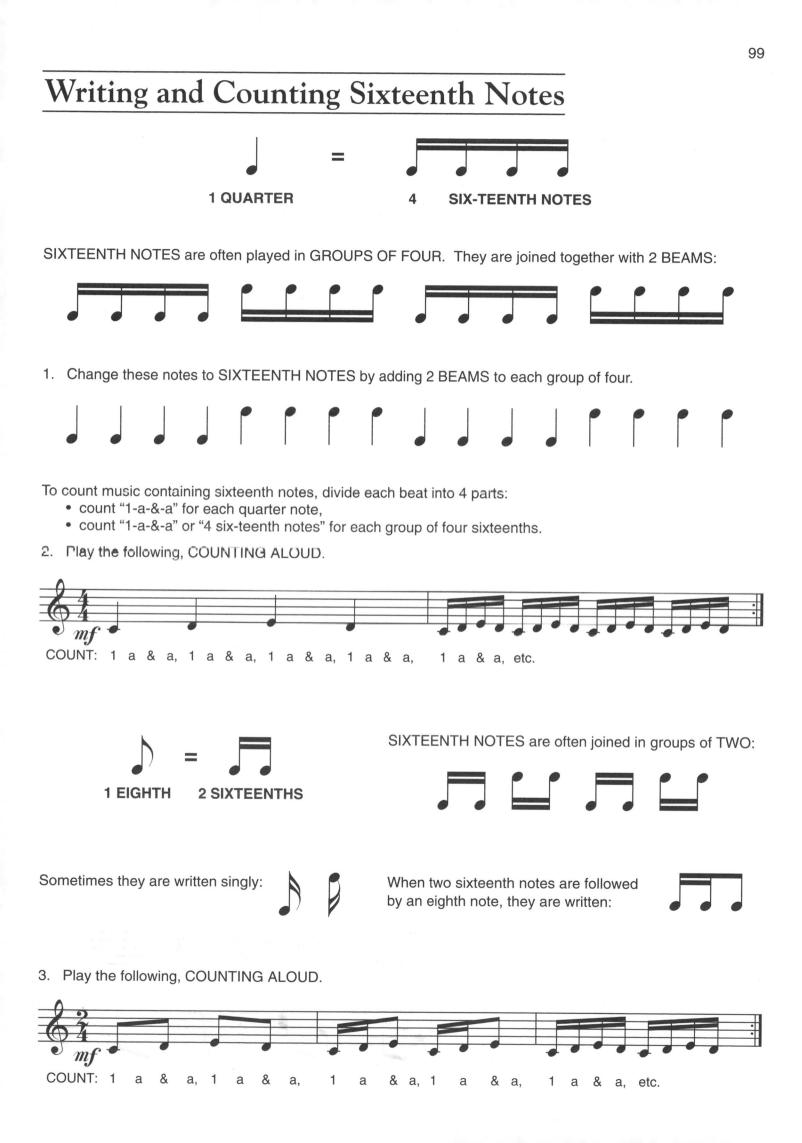

1 QUARTER   **4   SIX-TEENTH NOTES**

SIXTEENTH NOTES are often played in GROUPS OF FOUR. They are joined together with 2 BEAMS:

1.   Change these notes to SIXTEENTH NOTES by adding 2 BEAMS to each group of four.

To count music containing sixteenth notes, divide each beat into 4 parts:
  • count "1-a-&-a" for each quarter note,
  • count "1-a-&-a" or "4 six-teenth notes" for each group of four sixteenths.

2.   Play the following, COUNTING ALOUD.

COUNT: 1 a & a, 1 a & a, 1 a & a, 1 a & a,   1 a & a, etc.

1 EIGHTH   2 SIXTEENTHS

SIXTEENTH NOTES are often joined in groups of TWO:

Sometimes they are written singly:

When two sixteenth notes are followed by an eighth note, they are written:

3.   Play the following, COUNTING ALOUD.

COUNT: 1 a & a 1 a & a,   1 a & a, 1 a & a,   1 a & a, etc.

Leopold Mozart was not only famous for nurturing the phenomenal talent of his son, Wolfgang Amadeus Mozart, but also for having been an excellent composer, a renowned violinist, and court composer in the service of the Archbishop of Salzburg, Austria.

BOURLESQ* 🔊44)))

Leopold Mozart

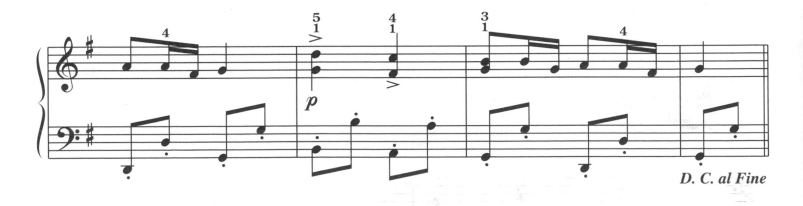

Bourlesq = Old French spelling for "burlesque," a playful or comical dance.

ARKANSAS TRAVELER

American Folk Tune

Allegro moderato

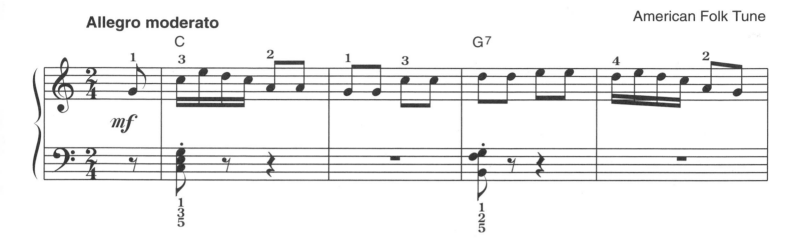

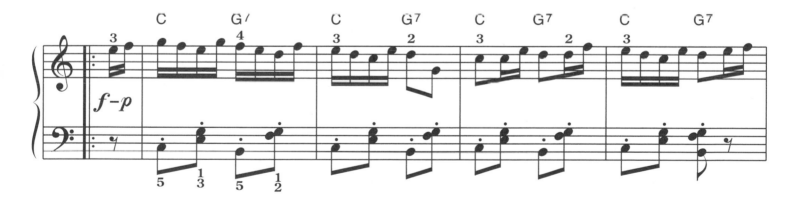

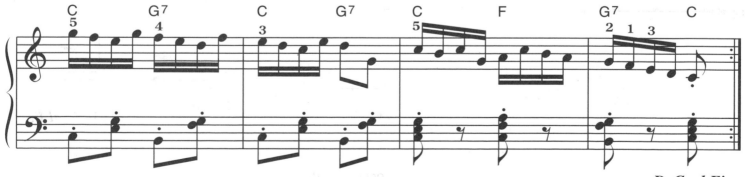

D. C. al Fine

Theme from MUSETTA'S WALTZ

(from "La Bohème")

Giacomo Puccini

Moderately slow

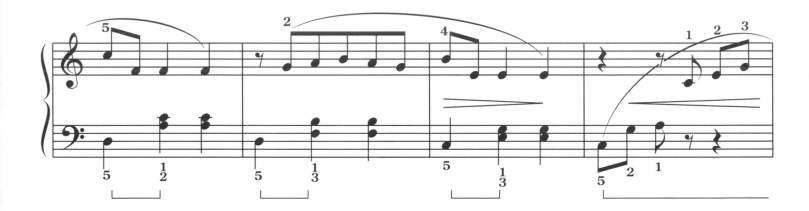

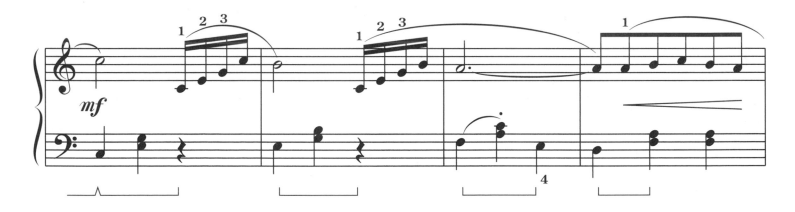

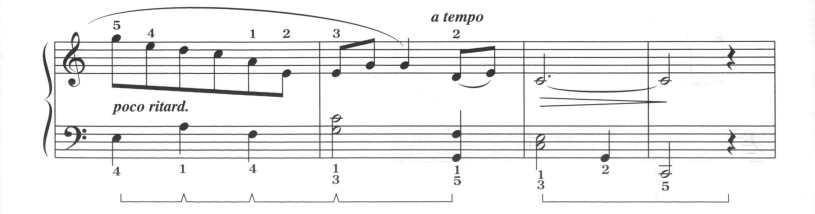

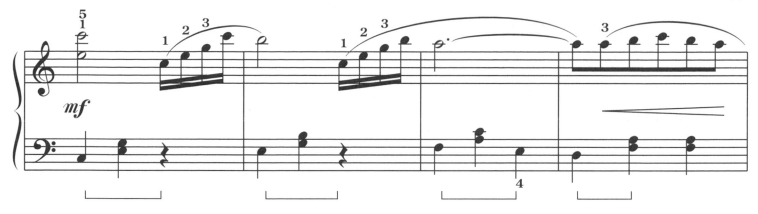

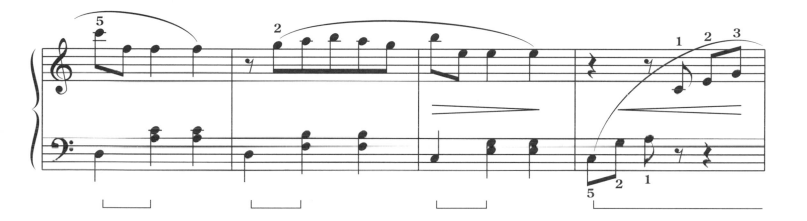

The Dotted Eighth Note

A DOTTED EIGHTH NOTE has the same value as an eighth note tied to a sixteenth note.

Count aloud and play:

COUNT: 1 a & a   etc.

The following line should sound exactly the same as the above line.
The only difference is the way it is written.

COUNT: 1 a & a   etc.

THE BATTLE HYMN OF THE REPUBLIC

Slow march tempo

Steffe-Howe

Maestoso

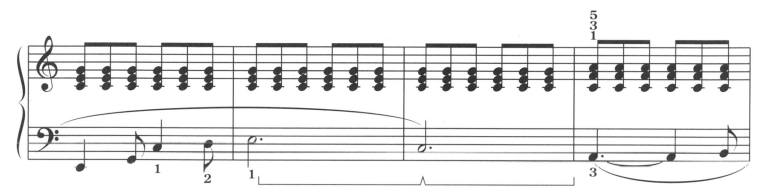

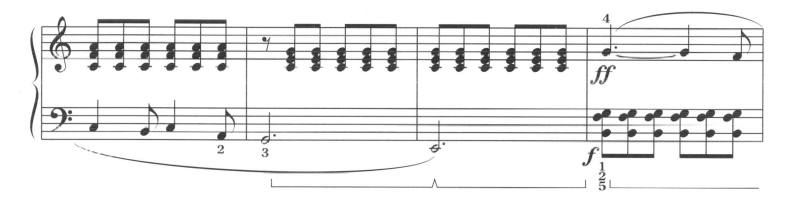

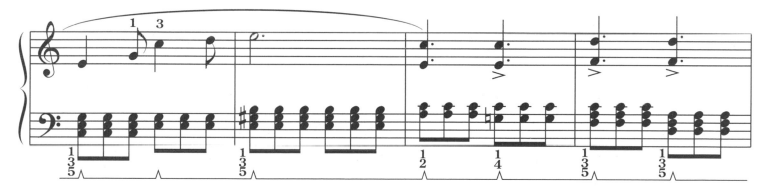

106

The B♭ Major Scale

REMEMBER! The MAJOR SCALE is made of TWO TETRACHORDS joined by a WHOLE STEP.
The pattern of each tetrachord is: WHOLE STEP—WHOLE STEP—HALF STEP.

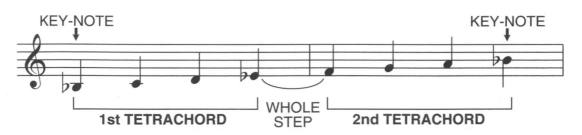

The fingering for the B♭ MAJOR SCALE is irregular. The 5th finger is not used in either hand.
The RH plays the key note, B♭, with the 4th finger. The fingering groups then fall
1 2 3 - 1 2 3 4 ascending, then 4 3 2 1 - 3 2 1 descending, ending on 4.

Play slowly and carefully!

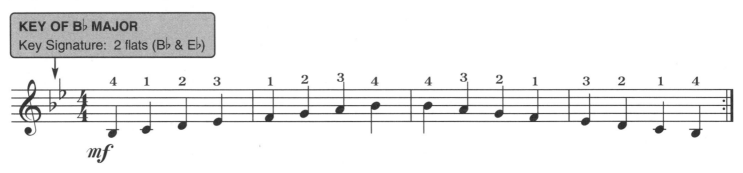

The LH plays the key note, B♭, with the 3rd finger. The fingering groups then fall
1 2 3 4 - 1 2 3 descending, then 3 2 1 - 4 3 2 1 ascending, ending on 3.

Play slowly and carefully!

THE RIDDLE

The popular song "The Twelfth of Never" was based on this well-known folk melody.

Folk Song

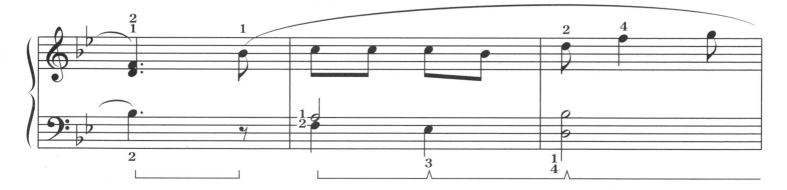

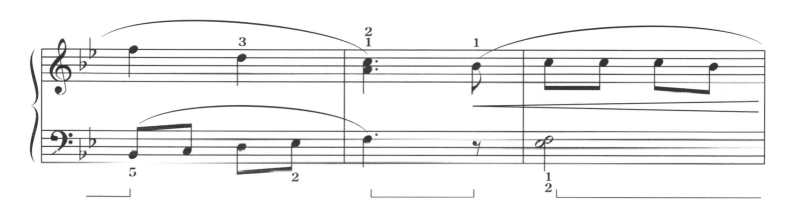

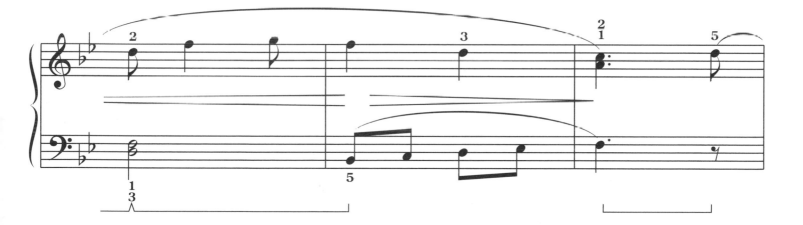

Writing in the Key of B♭ Major

1. Write the letter names of the notes of the B♭ MAJOR SCALE, from *left to right*, on the keyboard below. Be sure the WHOLE STEPS & HALF STEPS are correct!

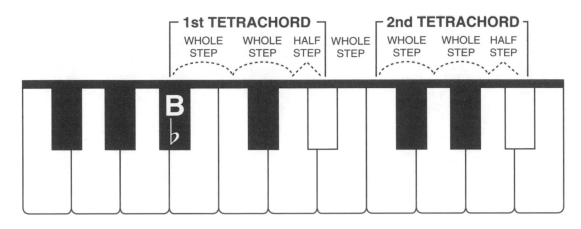

2. Check to be sure you wrote E♭ as the 4th note of the scale. It cannot be called D♯, because scale notes are always in alphabetical order. (You cannot have a scale with two D's and no E's!)

3. Complete the tetrachord beginning on B♭. Write one note over each finger number.

4. Complete the tetrachord beginning on F. Write one note over each finger number.

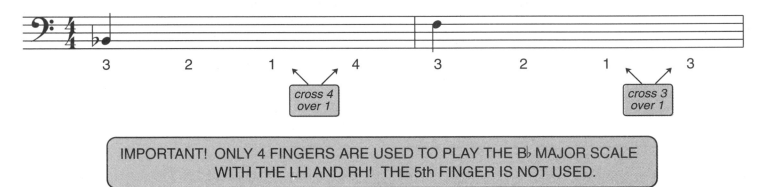

IMPORTANT! ONLY 4 FINGERS ARE USED TO PLAY THE B♭ MAJOR SCALE WITH THE LH AND RH! THE 5th FINGER IS NOT USED.

Beginning with LH 3, the scale is fingered in groups of 3 2 1 - 4 3 2 1 ascending.

5. Write the fingering UNDER each note of the following LH scale.   6. Play with LH.

KEY OF B♭ MAJOR
Key Signature: 2 flats (B♭ & E♭)

Beginning with RH 4, the fingering groups that follow are 1 2 3 - 1 2 3 4 ascending.

7. Write the finger OVER each note of the following RH scale.   8. Play with RH.

THE MAGIC PIPER

Allegro moderato

The Primary Chords in B♭ Major

Reviewing the B♭ MAJOR SCALE, LH ascending.

KEY OF B♭ MAJOR
Key Signature: 2 flats (B♭ & E♭)

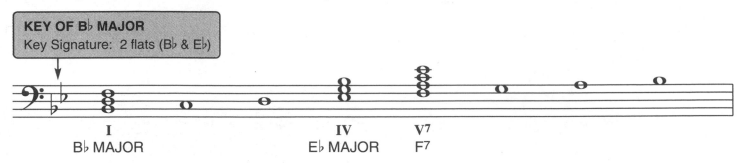

The following positions are often used for smooth progressions:

B♭ Major Chord Progression with I, IV & V7 chords.

Play several times, saying the chord names and numerals aloud:

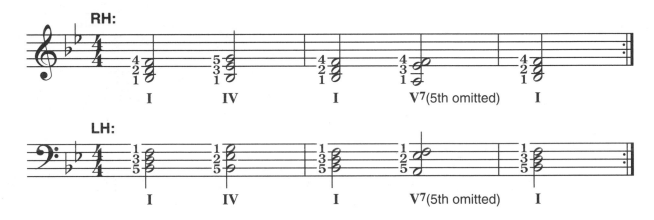

HE'S GOT THE WHOLE WORLD IN HIS HANDS

Moderately and rhythmically

Spiritual

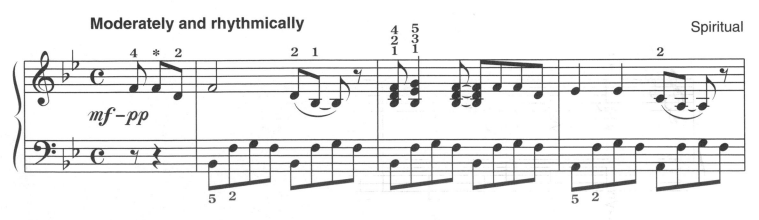

*Play pairs of eighth notes a bit unevenly, long-short.

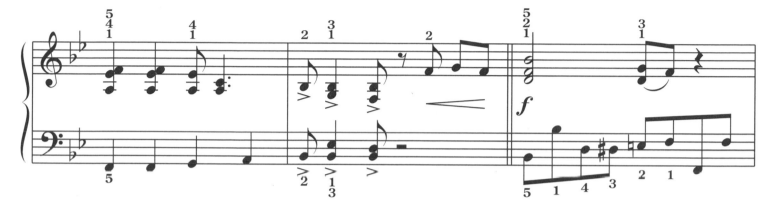

D. C. al ⊕, then CODA

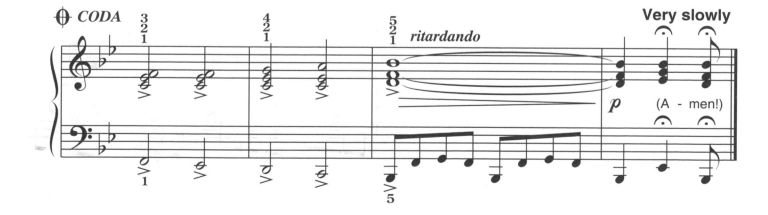

BALLIN' THE JACK*

Words by Jim Burris
Music by Chris Smith

Not too fast

First you put your two knees close up tight, Then you

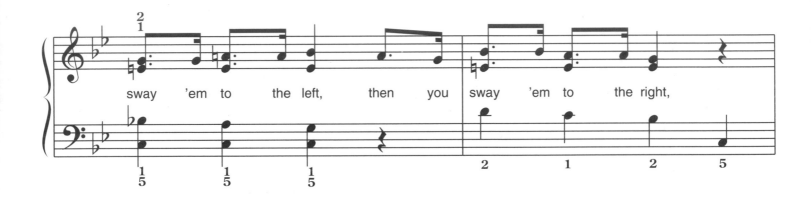

sway 'em to the left, then you sway 'em to the right,

Step a-round the floor kind of nice and light, Then you

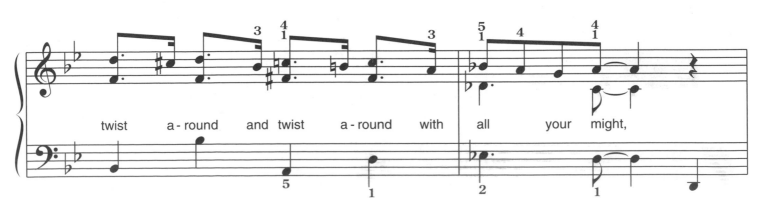

twist a-round and twist a-round with all your might,

*All rights outside the United States controlled by Edward B. Marks Music Company.

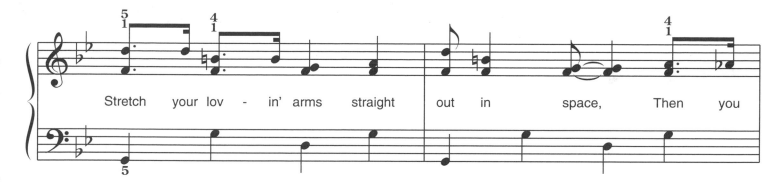

Stretch your lov - in' arms straight out in space, Then you

do the Ea - gle Rock with style and grace, Swing your

foot way 'round then bring it back, Now that's what I call

1. "Ball - in' the Jack!"   2. "Ball - in' the Jack!"

Writing the Primary Chords in B♭ Major

KEY OF B♭ MAJOR
Key Signature: 2 flats (B♭ & E♭)

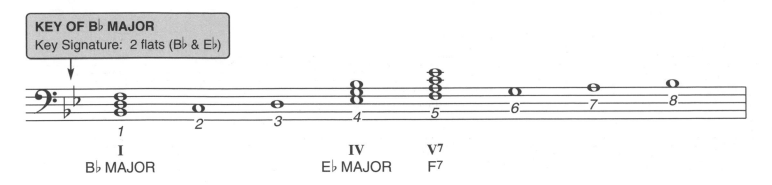

I			IV	V⁷
B♭ MAJOR			E♭ MAJOR	F⁷

These positions are often used for smooth progressions:

B♭ is the COMMON TONE between **I** & **IV**. **F** is the COMMON TONE between **I** & **V⁷**.

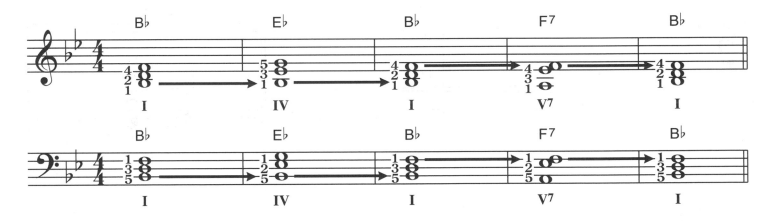

1. Rewrite the above progressions on the following staffs.
2. Add fingering.   3. Add arrows to show the common tones.   4. Play with hands separate.

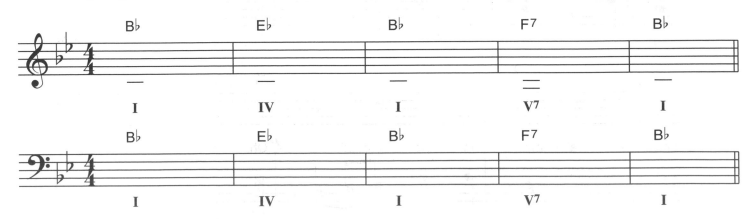

NOBODY KNOWS THE TROUBLE I'VE SEEN

Spiritual

LA DONNA E MOBILE

(from "Rigoletto")

This is one of the most popular operatic songs ever written. The rest in the 8th measure of the introduction must have come as quite a surprise at the first performance, and it still lends the piece a certain special charm. The entire piece may be played twice, right from the beginning, including the repeated two lines, since that is the way it is performed in the opera.

Allegro moderato

Giuseppe Verdi

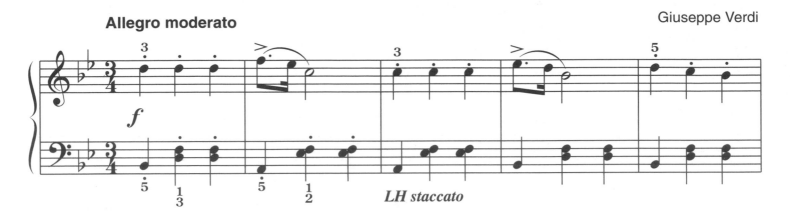

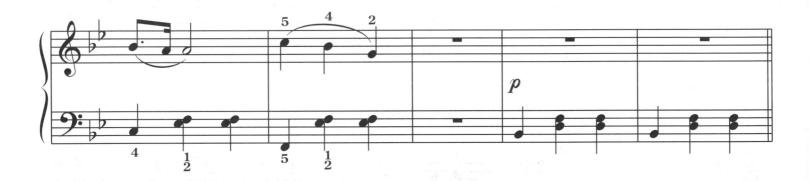

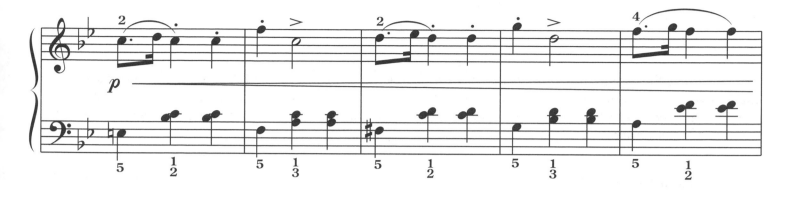

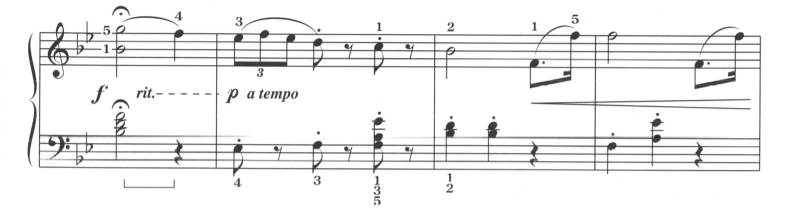

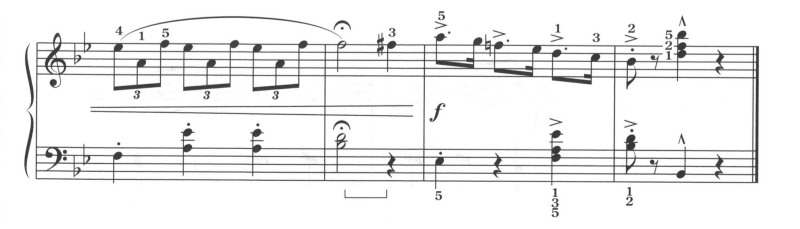

FRANKIE AND JOHNNIE

This "eight-to-the-bar" style is known as "Boogie Woogie." Play with a driving rhythm, with the eighth notes in long-short pairs. This is an excellent review in syncopation, and is fun to play.

Traditional

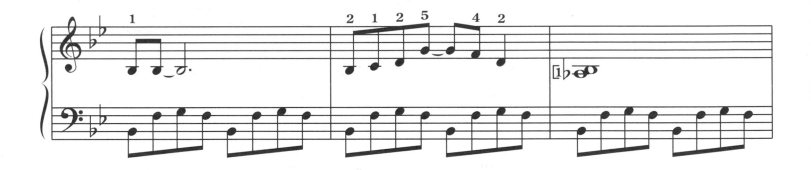

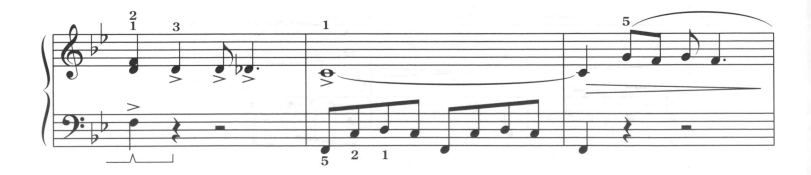

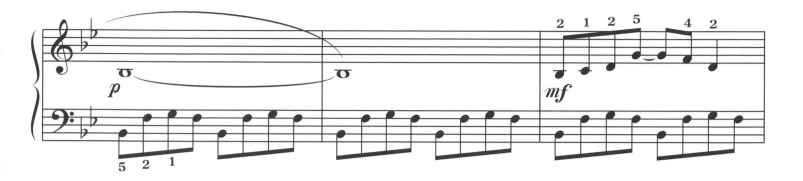

The Key of G Minor (Relative of B♭ Major)

G MINOR is the relative of **B♭ MAJOR**.

Both keys have the same key signature (2 flats, B♭ & E♭).

REMEMBER: The RELATIVE MINOR begins on the 6th tone of the MAJOR SCALE.

B♭ MAJOR SCALE

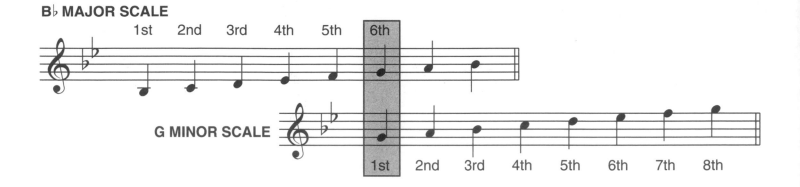

The minor scale shown above is called the NATURAL MINOR SCALE.

It uses only notes that are found in the relative major scale.

The G Harmonic Minor Scale

In the HARMONIC MINOR SCALE, the 7th tone is raised ascending and descending.

The raised 7th in the key of G MINOR is F♯. It is not included in the key signature,

but it is written as an "accidental" sharp each time it occurs.

Practice the G HARMONIC MINOR SCALE with hands separate. Begin slowly.

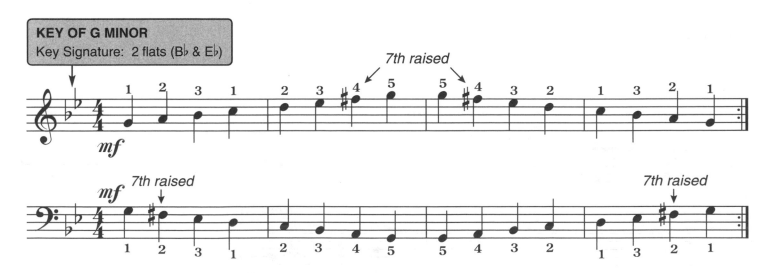

IMPORTANT!   After you have learned the G HARMONIC MINOR SCALE with hands separate, you may play
the hands together in CONTRARY MOTION, by combining the two staffs above.

BLACK IS THE COLOR OF MY TRUE LOVE'S HAIR

Folk Song

* // = *Caesura* (pronounced *say-ZHUR-ah,* but usually called "railroad tracks").
This indicates a momentary interruption of the melody with silence.

The Primary Chords in G Minor

Reviewing the G MINOR SCALE, LH ascending.

KEY OF G MINOR
Key Signature: 2 flats (B♭ & E♭)

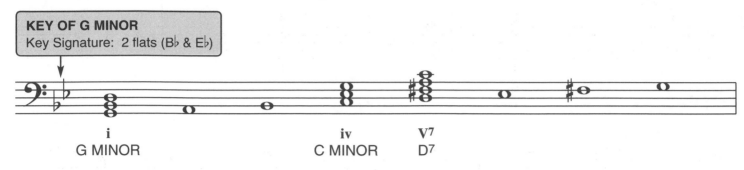

i		iv	V⁷	
G MINOR		C MINOR	D⁷	

The following positions are often used for smooth progressions:

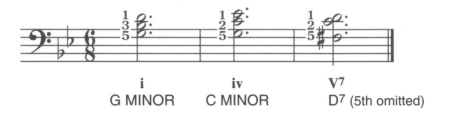

i	iv	V⁷
G MINOR	C MINOR	D⁷ (5th omitted)

G MINOR PROGRESSION with **i, iv** & **V⁷ chords.** Play several times.

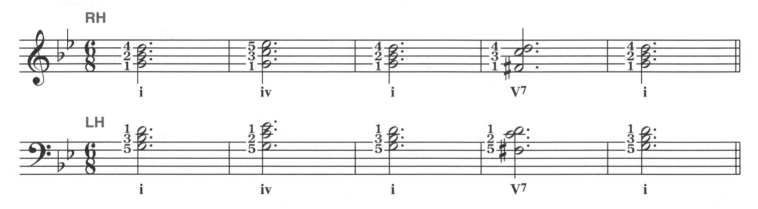

WHEN JOHNNY COMES MARCHING HOME 🔊

American Folk Song

March tempo

* A whole rest means *rest for a whole measure in ANY time signature.*

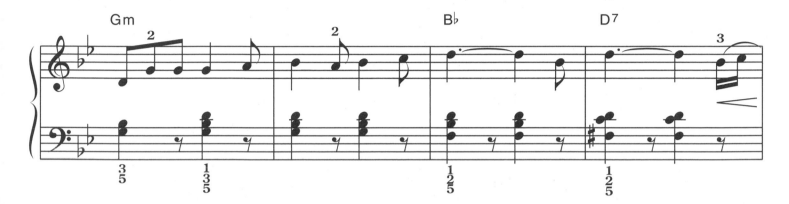

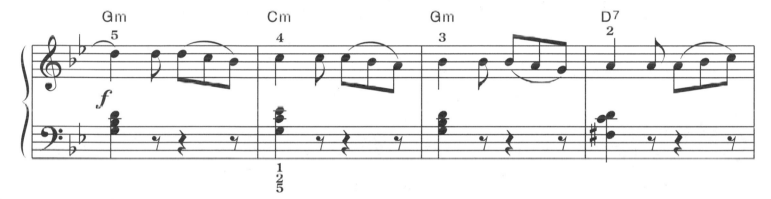

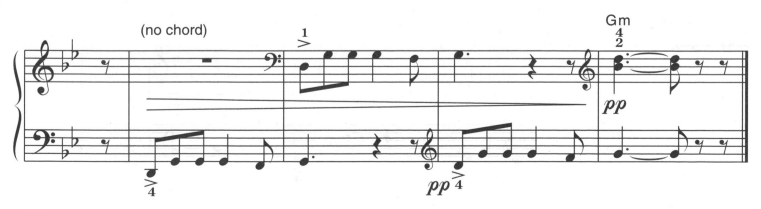

* This inversion of the B♭ MAJOR CHORD was used in the key of F MAJOR.

Writing the Primary Chords in G Minor

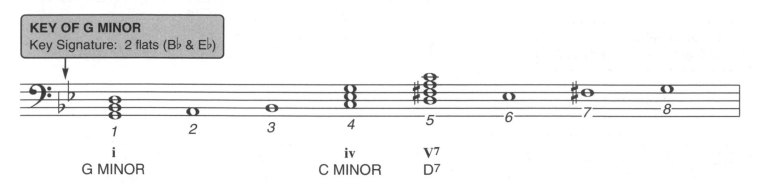

KEY OF G MINOR
Key Signature: 2 flats (B♭ & E♭)

1   2   3   4   5   6   7   8

i — G MINOR   iv — C MINOR   V⁷ — D⁷

The following positions are often used for smooth progressions:

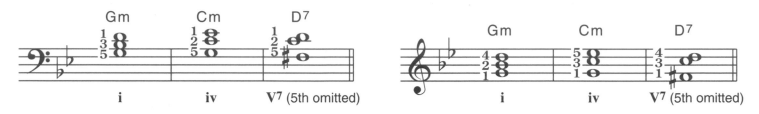

Gm   Cm   D⁷
i   iv   V⁷ (5th omitted)

Gm   Cm   D⁷
i   iv   V⁷ (5th omitted)

G is the COMMON TONE between **i** & **iv**.   **D** is the COMMON TONE between **i** & **V⁷**.

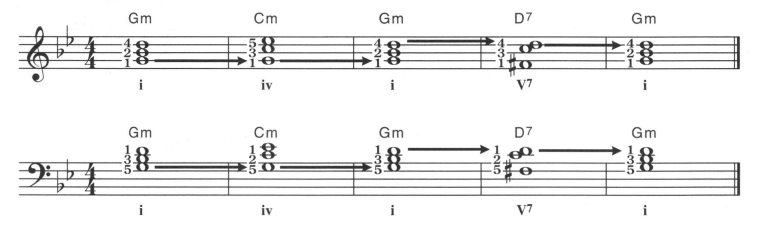

Gm   Cm   Gm   D⁷   Gm
i   iv   i   V⁷   i

Gm   Cm   Gm   D⁷   Gm
i   iv   i   V⁷   i

1. Rewrite the above progressions on the following staffs.
2. Add fingering.   3. Add arrows to show the common tones.   4. Play with hands separate.

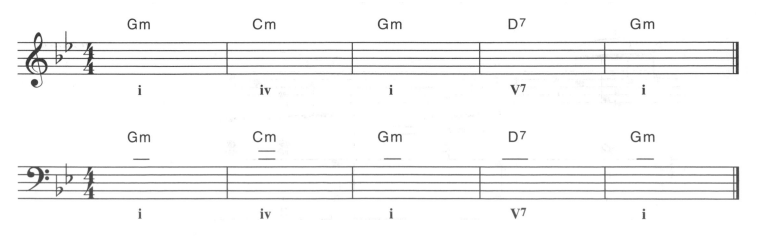

Gm   Cm   Gm   D⁷   Gm
i   iv   i   V⁷   i

Gm   Cm   Gm   D⁷   Gm
i   iv   i   V⁷   i

Waltz in G Minor

The third line of this piece is in B♭ MAJOR, the relative of G minor. The primary chords are reviewed with the same positions in RH and LH. The fourth line returns to G minor, with the primary chords of that key also in the same positions in RH and LH.

KEY OF G MINOR
Key Signature: 2 flats (B♭ & E♭)

Waltz tempo

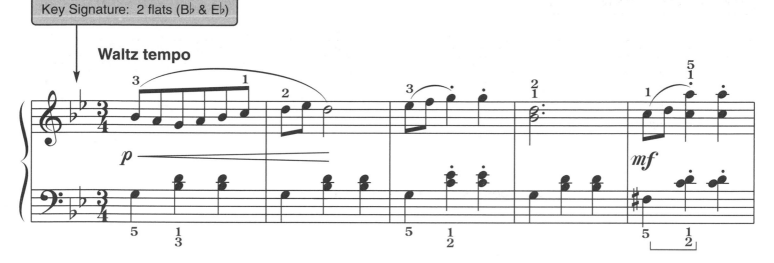

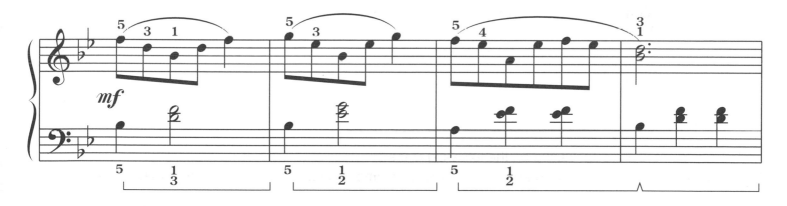

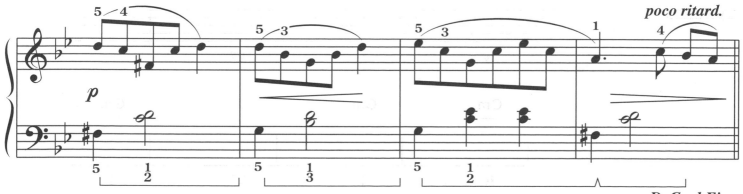

poco ritard.

D. C. al Fine

Reviewing: Major & Minor Triads

You have already learned the following:

MAJOR TRIADS consist of a
ROOT, MAJOR 3rd, & PERFECT 5th.

MINOR TRIADS consist of a
ROOT, MINOR 3rd, & PERFECT 5th.

C MAJOR TRIAD = **C MINOR TRIAD =**

Any MAJOR triad may be changed to a MINOR triad by LOWERING the 3rd ONE HALF STEP!

Play a MAJOR triad, then a MINOR triad, on each note of the C MAJOR SCALE. Begin as shown below.
Play with LH, using 5 3 1 on each triad. Repeat *8va* with RH, using 1 3 5.

etc.

Introducing: Diminished Triads

The word DIMINISHED means "made smaller."
When a PERFECT 5th is made smaller by one half step, it becomes a DIMINISHED 5th.
A DIMINISHED TRIAD consists of a ROOT, MINOR 3rd, & DIMINISHED 5th.

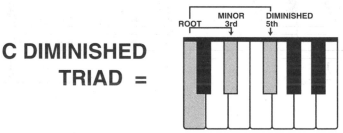

C DIMINISHED TRIAD =

IMPORTANT!
It is helpful to note
that the interval between
each note of a DIMINISHED
TRIAD is **3 HALF STEPS!**

Any MINOR triad may be changed to a DIMINISHED triad by LOWERING the 5th ONE HALF STEP!

Play a MINOR triad, then a DIMINISHED triad, on each note of the C MAJOR SCALE. Begin as shown below.
Play with LH, using 5 3 1 on each triad. Repeat *8va* with RH, using 1 3 5. The symbol for the diminished triad
is **dim** (or ○).

etc.

Any MAJOR triad may be changed to a DIMINISHED triad by LOWERING the 3rd & 5th ONE HALF STEP!

Play a MAJOR triad, then a DIMINISHED triad, on each note of the C MAJOR SCALE. Begin as shown
below. Play with LH, using 5 3 1 on each triad. Repeat *8va* with RH, using 1 3 5.

etc.

Theme from SYMPHONY NO. 6 (1st MOVEMENT)

This expressive theme from Peter Ilyich Tchaikovsky's 6th Symphony, known as "The Pathetique Symphony,"
was the basis for a popular song.

Tchaikovsky

Play these measures several times to prepare for *FASCINATION.*

Fingering C chord with 4 2 1 makes
reaching down to G easier.

Play the 2nd (F & G) with
the side of the thumb!

FASCINATION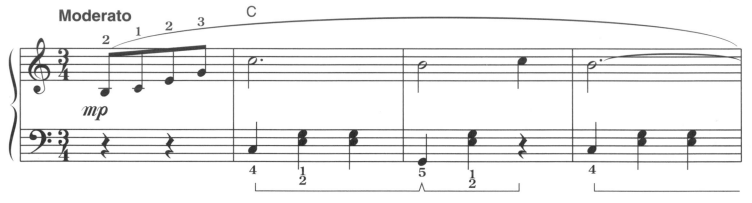

F. Marchetti

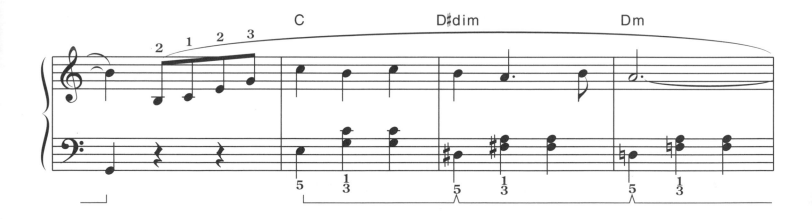

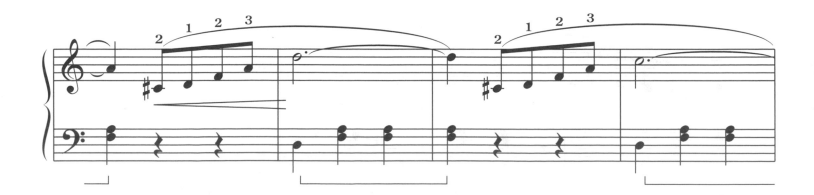

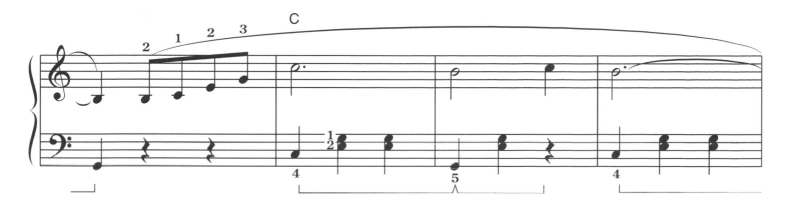

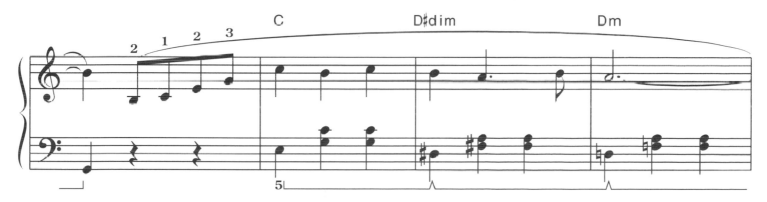

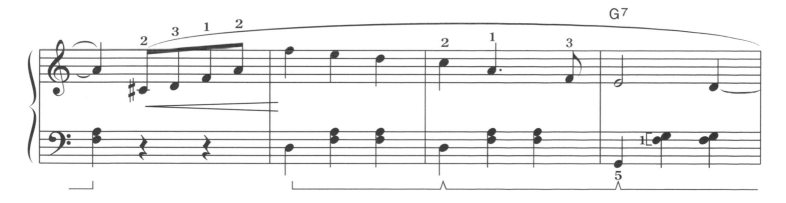

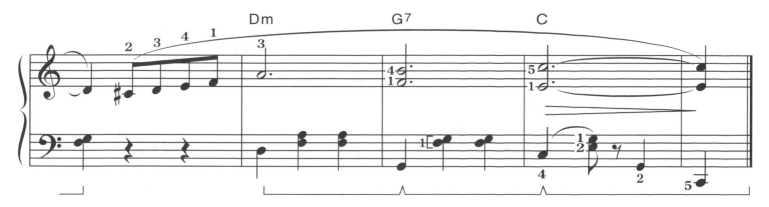

Introducing: Augmented Triads

The word AUGMENTED means "made larger."
When a PERFECT 5th is made larger by one
half step, it becomes an AUGMENTED 5th.

An AUGMENTED TRIAD consists of a ROOT,
MAJOR 3rd, & AUGMENTED 5th.

AUGMENTED TRIAD =

Any MAJOR triad may be changed to an AUGMENTED triad by raising the 5th ONE HALF STEP!

C MAJOR C AUGMENTED F MAJOR F AUGMENTED G MAJOR G AUGMENTED

Play a MAJOR triad, then an AUGMENTED triad, on each note of the C MAJOR SCALE, as shown below.
Play very slowly with LH, using 5 3 1 on each triad. Repeat *8va* with RH, using 1 3 5. The symbol for the
augmented triad is **aug** (or **+**).

C C aug D D aug E E aug F F aug

G G aug A A aug B B aug C C aug

DOUBLE SHARP (✗)
Raises a sharped note another half step,
or a natural note one whole step.

DEEP RIVER 🔊 58

Adagio moderato

Traditional

Deep   Riv - er,   My   home   is   o - ver

C   C aug   F   C   Am

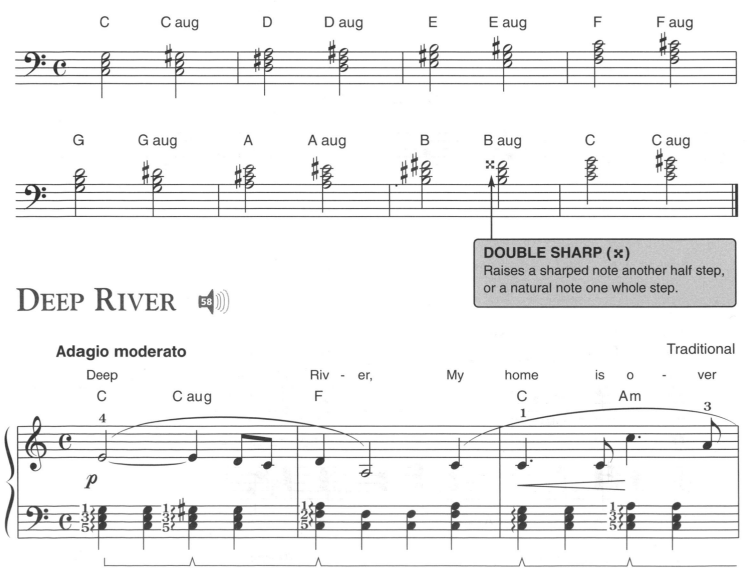

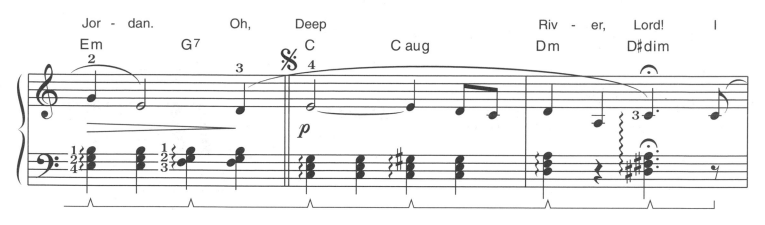

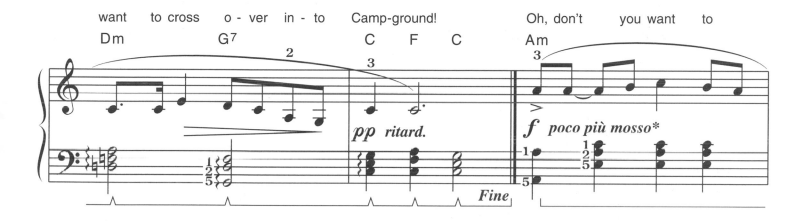

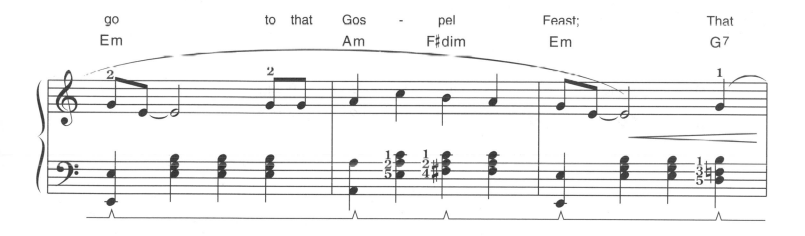

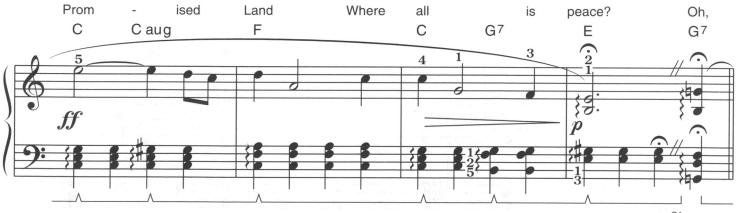

D. S. 𝄋 al Fine

*Poco più mosso = a little faster.

(Repeat from the sign 𝄋, and play to the Fine.)

The E♭ Major Scale

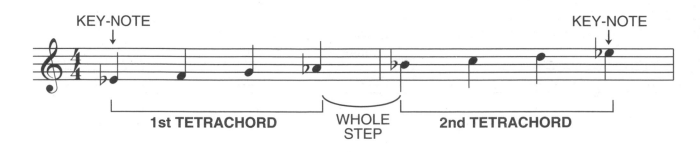

The 5th finger is not used in either hand in the E♭ MAJOR SCALE.
The key note, E♭, is played by the 3rd finger of the RH and the LH.

Play slowly and carefully!

KEY OF E♭ MAJOR
Key Signature: 3 flats (B♭, E♭, & A♭)

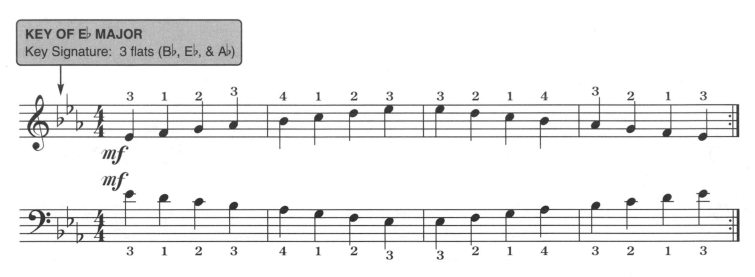

After you have learned to play the E♭ MAJOR SCALE with hands separate,
you may play the hands together in contrary motion. Both hands play the
same numbered fingers at the same time!

LOCH LOMOND

Traditional

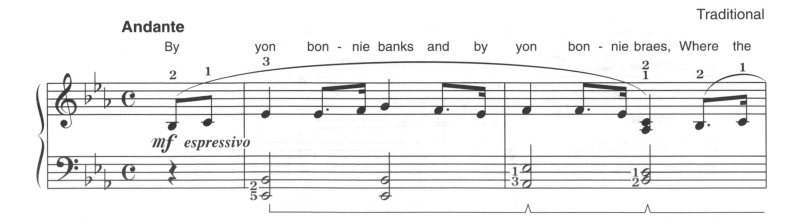

sun shines bright on Loch Lo - mond, Where me and my true love were

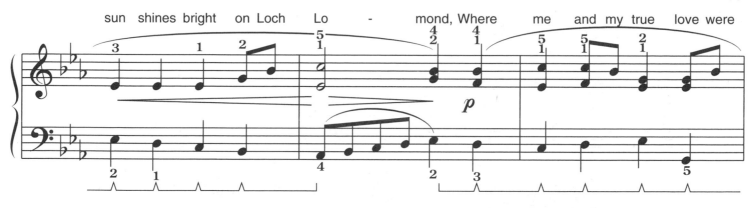

ev - er wont to be, On the bon - nie, bon - nie banks of Loch Lo - mond.

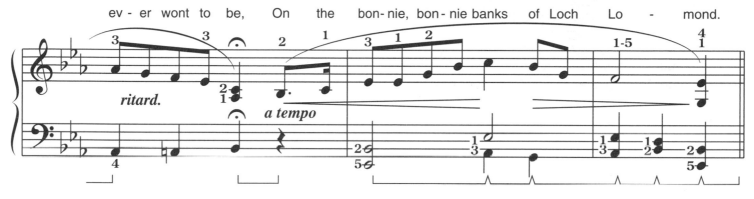

Risoluto*

Oh, you'll take the high road and I'll take the low road, And

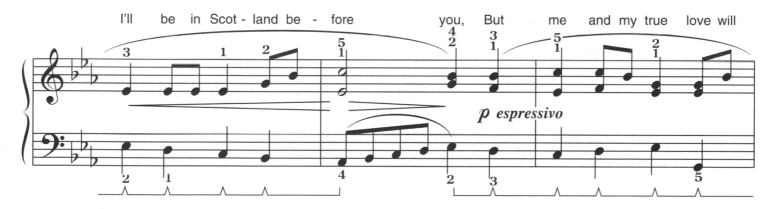

I'll be in Scot - land be - fore you, But me and my true love will

nev - er meet a - gain, On the bon - nie, bon - nie banks of Loch Lo - mond.

*Risoluto = resolutely.

Writing in the Key of E♭ Major

1. Write the letter names of the notes of the E♭ MAJOR SCALE, from *left to right,* on the keyboard below. Be sure the WHOLE STEPS & HALF STEPS are correct!

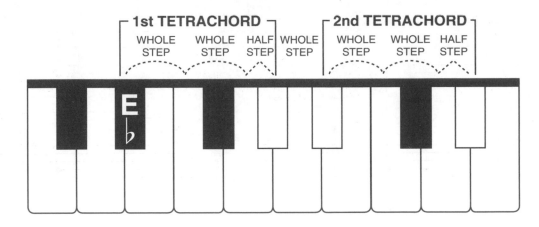

2. Check to be sure that you wrote A♭ as the 4th note of the scale, and B♭ as the 5th note. These notes cannot be called G♯ and A♯ because scale notes must always be named in alphabetical order. (You cannot have two G's and no A's, or two A's and no B's!)

3. Complete the tetrachord beginning on E♭. Write one note over each finger number.

4. Complete the tetrachord beginning on B♭. Write one note over each finger number.

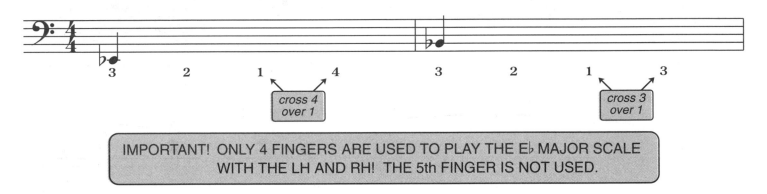

IMPORTANT! ONLY 4 FINGERS ARE USED TO PLAY THE E♭ MAJOR SCALE WITH THE LH AND RH! THE 5th FINGER IS NOT USED.

Beginning with LH 3, the scale is fingered in groups of 3 2 1 - 4 3 2 1; end on 3.

5. Write the fingering UNDER each note of the following LH scale.

6. Play with LH.

KEY OF E♭ MAJOR
Key Signature: 3 flats (B♭, E♭ & A♭)

After beginning with RH 3, the finger groups then fall 1 2 3 4 - 1 2 3.

7. Write the fingering OVER each note of the following RH scale.

8. Play with RH.

LOVE'S GREETING
(Salut d'amour)

Sir Edward Elgar
Arr. by Allan Small

Andantino grazioso

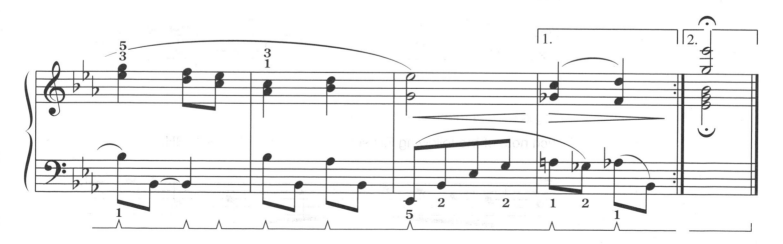

The Primary Chords in E♭ Major

Reviewing the E♭ MAJOR SCALE, LH ascending.

KEY OF E♭ MAJOR
Key Signature: 3 flats (B♭, E♭ & A♭)

I
E♭ MAJOR

IV
A♭ MAJOR

V⁷
B♭⁷

The following positions are often used, for smooth progressions:

I
E♭ MAJOR

IV
A♭ MAJOR

V⁷
B♭⁷ (5th omitted)

E♭ MAJOR CHORD PROGRESSION with I, IV & V⁷ chords.

Play with RH as written, then with LH one octave lower.

E♭ MAJOR PROGRESSION with broken I, IV & V⁷ chords. Play several times with LH.

The next piece contains the E♭ MAJOR TRIAD in ALL POSITIONS.
Practice the following as a warm-up exercise.

RH: BLOCK CHORDS

Root position · 1st inversion · 2nd inversion

RH: BROKEN CHORDS

Root position · 1st inversion · 2nd inversion

LH: BLOCK CHORDS

Root position · 1st inversion · 2nd inversion

LH: BROKEN CHORDS

Root position · 1st inversion · 2nd inversion

Aria from "THE MARRIAGE OF FIGARO"

This famous aria is prominently featured in the film, "Amadeus."

W. A. Mozart

Andante maestoso

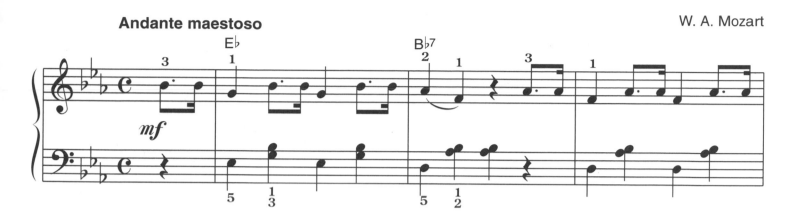

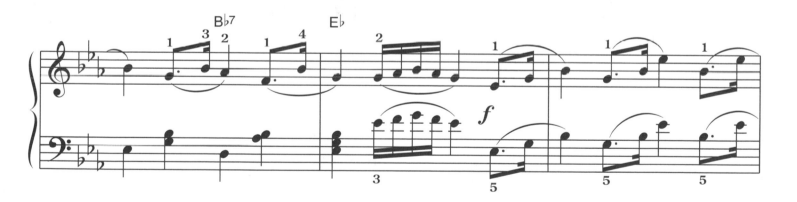

DANNY BOY

Words by Fred E. Weatherly
Adapted from an Old Irish Air

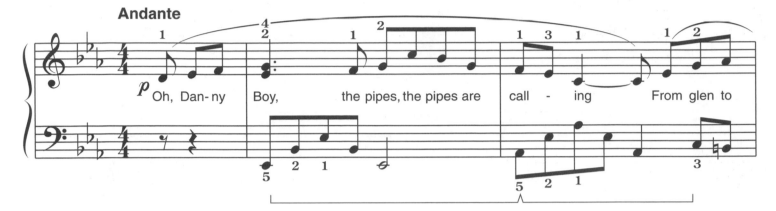

Oh, Dan- ny Boy, the pipes, the pipes are call - ing From glen to

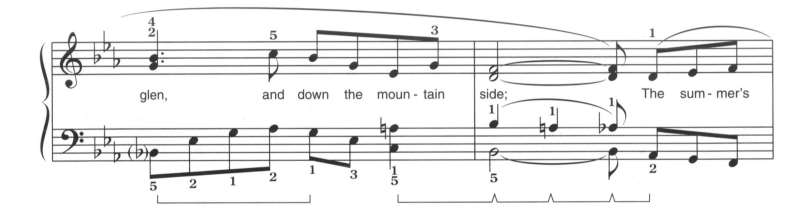

glen, and down the moun - tain side; The sum - mer's

gone, and all the ros - es fall - ing, It's you, it's

you must go, and I must bide.

PREPARATION FOR THE FOLLOWING PIECE

All the variations in the RH are based on this chord progression. Play it several times
before beginning the piece. Also play the LH of the piece several times.

VARIATIONS ON THE THEME FROM THE CELEBRATED CANON IN D

Pachelbel's *CANON IN D* was used as background in the film "Ordinary People," and has been heard in many
different settings, in supermarkets, movies, radio and television productions. Everywhere!

Pachelbel

Andante moderato

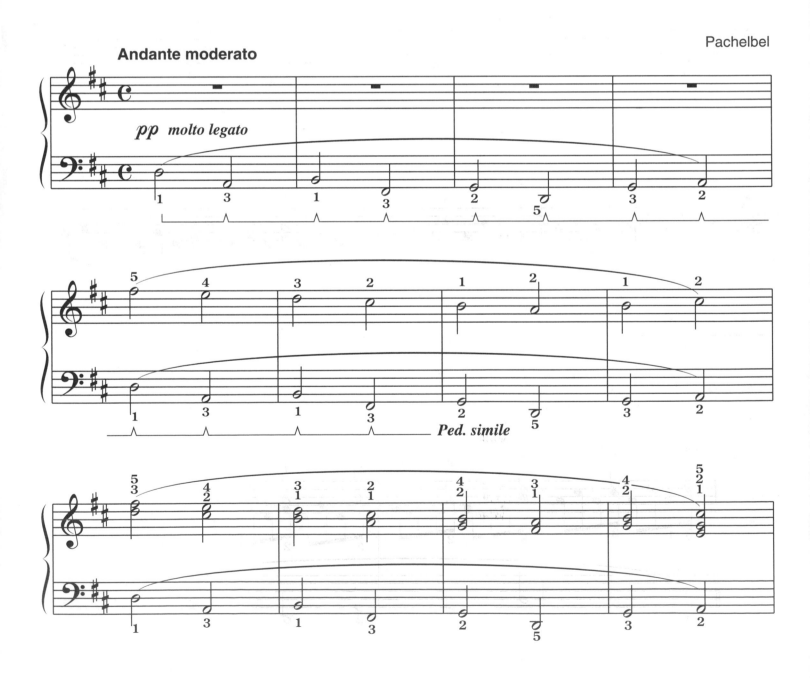

Ped. simile

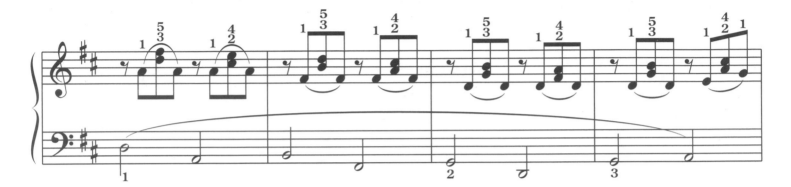

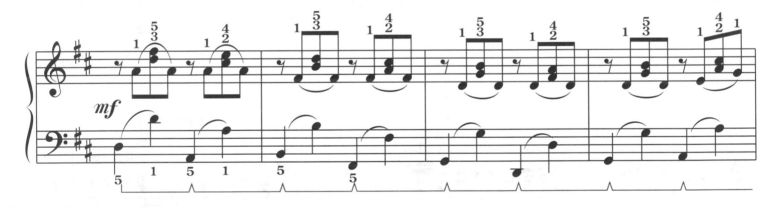

Slower

Still slower

poco ritard.

Maestoso

poco ritard.

ff

molto allargando

Certificate of Award

This is to certify that

has successfully completed

Alfred's Adult All-in-One Course, Level 2

and is hereby promoted to

Alfred's Basic Adult Course, Lesson Book 3.

Date

Teacher